THE FIFTH WEEK

THE FIFTH WEEK

William J. O'Malley, S.J.

LOYOLA UNIVERSITY PRESS
Chicago 60657

To my Jesuit brothers—
past, present, and to come—
who feed me more than three times a day.

© 1976 Loyola University Press

Printed in the United States of America

LIBRARY OF CONGRESS
CATALOGING IN PUBLICATION DATA

O'Malley, William J
  The fifth week.
  Bibliography: p.
  1. Jesuits—Biography. 2. Jesuits. I. Title.

BX3755.O65   271'.53'022[B]   75-43583

ISBN 0-8294-0248-9   Cover by Deborah Brown

Contents

Part Two Jesuits of the Present

Part Three Jesuits of the Future

Like many poets, Ignatius had an incisive sense of reality. He saw the Church needed men of common sense, practical men who saw what Christ wanted of them and who could find the best means to do it. Men not bound to some outworn shibboleth or unexamined, unnecessary custom but alive with the divine common sense and practical wisdom of the Holy Spirit within the Church: to couple the two forces within him--the poet's vision and the practical man's grasp of affairs and detail.

All that was visionary, mystical, imaginative and heroic in him must be preserved and put at Christ's service, but it must first be controlled, directed and given point by the prudence of God. He must blend and temper his magnanimity with prudence, that loveliest of virtues which makes all things real.

John C. Kelly, S.J.
"The Making of Ignatius"

Introduction

I think that . . . we must give them a very clear idea of vocation, that is of the Society as an ideal. But we must also give a clear idea of the Society today, of the real Society, so that they cannot ever say they have been deceived. . . . Explain the ideal Society, but also the limitations with which they will have to live.

> Pedro Arrupe, S.J.
> General of the Society of Jesus

Fortunately I resisted the temptation to call this book The Paradise Men's Club. In so doing, I also resisted the feeling that I ought to write one of those Gosh-Fellas-Do-We-Jesuits-Ever-Have-Fun! books. Some books on religious orders picture seminary life as if it were neatly divided between basketball courts enclosed by woodsy places and library tables hemmed in by intimidating bookshelves and huge crucifixes.

In short, I would like this book to be an honest picture of what being a Jesuit means, as far as I have seen and experienced it. While I was writing it I envisioned two different audiences. On the one hand, as John Cogley once said, "Every little movement has a Jebbie all its own." We turn up with disturbing regularity in the public press, storming some barricade or other--and most often there is some Jesuit publicly defending the very barricade that other Jesuits are attacking. Consequently all kinds of people--Protestants, Jews, nonbelievers, even other Catholics--keep wondering, "What makes these puzzling men tick?" This book is, in part, an attempt to answer their question.

The other audience is the group of young men who are considering the Society as a way of life for them. They feel some sort of attraction to the life of a Jesuit and wonder just what they'd be letting themselves in for if they took definite steps to apply. As Father Arrupe says above, it would be a cruel disservice not only to those men but to the Society to offer such men a false picture of Jesuit life. Therefore, I have tried to show us as we are, warts and all. Hopefully, this book, especially the later chapters, will be of some help in showing them what Jesuits are like.

Like other men, each Jesuit is unique. We have fat ones and skinny ones, white ones and black ones, ordained and waiting to be ordained and never to be ordained ones. We have brilliant, eager, selfless Jesuits and, to be honest, we also have lazy, dulled, fearful Jesuits, and a great many in between the two dramatic extremes. There is no such thing as a "Jesuit mold" which turns us out like identical lead soldiers. On the other hand, however, there is a great core of realizations which every Jesuit, despite his unique person or work or generation, shares with all his brother Jesuits. Most people who know us will agree that the experience we all have had of the Spiritual Exercises of St. Ignatius gives a particular coloration to a Jesuit. It lasts his whole life. Each of us has made this intense thirty-day retreat at least once, and that experience not only shaped our way of thinking but it also taught us a com-

mon language which sometimes makes non-Jesuits feel mys-
tified.

Jesuit priests have also shared a common course of studies:
from novitiate, through a heavily classical and philosophical
college program, through teaching, through theological studies
and ordination into ministerial work. The Jesuit who plies an
outrigger in the South Pacific and the Jesuit who frames legis-
lation in Congress and the Jesuit who does biblical research in
Jerusalem have all had the same basic training for ten years.
As a result I can sit down in Milwaukee or North Wales or
Moscow and have a beer with Jesuits I've never met and know
that we already have a wealth of shared experience.

But it goes further than that. One Jesuit, I think, put it well:
"A man becomes a Jesuit by associating with other Jesuits." It
means living very, very closely with men who not only have
shared the Spiritual Exercises and the training, but who have
shared the living out of those ideals in the world. Different
Jesuits have different politics, different life-styles, different
interests; but as Jesuits they all focus primarily on two facets
of the gospel message, Jesus Christ has come to set us free
and to make us more alive.

This living with other Jesuits is not restricted, though, to
the Jesuits a man can shake hands with in his twenty or forty
or sixty years. It includes the biggies too. I am somehow amplified by my brother Jesuits like Bob Drinan and John McLaughlin,
Dan Berrigan and Dan Lyons, Nick Weber and Swami Anima-
nanda. I may disagree with them. Their work may be so complex I don't understand it But somehow I am amplified by them.

Further, this association with other Jesuits is not even re-
stricted to the living. My Jesuitness is enriched by the fact that
I share it with Ignatius and Xavier and Clavius, with Robert de
Nobili and the North American Martyrs, with Bellarmine and
Canisius, with LeLubac and Chardin and John Courtney Murray.
All the Jesuits of the past 450 years are also my brothers.

This book, then, will be an attempt to show what being a
Jesuit means, and in doing so, what finding, accepting, and
living a vocation means.

3

Part I, Jesuits of the Past, is not intended to be another of those historical background ploys which one is obliged to plow through just to get "the full scoop." It is a study of the vocation of the first Jesuit, Ignatius Loyola, the vocation of the Society of Jesus, and the vocations of men who were inspired by the vision of Ignatius.

Throughout these pages the reader will begin to discover that a vocation is patterned. There is a certain rhythm that every vocation follows no matter where or when: the first reluctant stirrings and fumblings, the decisive meeting with God which makes a man stand up and walk, and the life journeys in which that meeting is lived out, amplified, fulfilled.

A vocation is also infectious. The vocation of Ignatius became the Society of Jesus. And the vocation of the Society gave rise to the vocations of the great Jesuits described in the second chapter and one hundred thousand others. The vocation of Ignatius, the vocation of the Society, and the vocations of each of its men began a cross-feeding back and forth: the men made an act of faith in the Society and the Society made an act of faith in them; the Society transformed the men and the men transformed the Society.

Part II, Jesuits of the Present, shows how that same vocation, discovered by a Basque petty officer at the behest of a cannonball in the 16th century, has been discovered, chosen, and lived again in the 20th century by some men who did it superlatively. But not all men are heroes, and one can learn only so much about the genesis of a vocation from a man's living it out publicly. Therefore the second half of Part II exchanges the telescope for the microscope and shows an ordinary vocation, my own, and how it grew step by weary and joyful step, from the inside. Moreover, in showing the unnewsworthy ups and downs of my own vocation, I will be able to give some feeling of the Jesuit course of studies and some notion of the ordinary and unnewsworthy men whose greatness formed whatever Jesuitness I have today. It is these men, anonymous to history, who are the Society of Jesus, yesterday, today, and tomorrow.

4

Part III, Jesuits of the Future, attempts to show how a vocation might begin and grow today. It attempts to show the real Society a man will enter and the world from which he must emerge. The secularism of the world challenges the Society and its men to offer a meaningful alternative to its materialist promises. In such a world, how does a man decide what Ignatius decided: to be a priest, to be a religious, to be a Jesuit? Then, if a man makes that decision, what does he do?

Ignatius, the battle-shattered worldling, had a long journey from a dream of courtly accomplishments to the reality of being father to one hundred thousand Jesuits. The young man today has an equally long journey through the thickets of Madison Avenue promises, past the sirens of success, to the rather ordinary door of the Jesuit novitiate. But no matter what the current dissuasions, no matter who the man or what the era, the journey is the same.

Jesuits of the Past

St. Ignatius Loyola, 1491-1556

Valiantly brave, unselfish, courtly and blissfully foolish, Don
Quixote vowed to defend the oppressed and protect the innocent.
He moved toward an ideal past where there was no greed,
where "those two fatal words 'thine' and 'mine' were distinctions unknown," where men needed only to be shown true friendship and love, and the Kingdom of Eden would automatically
return to the earth. And so he set off in pursuit of the Impossible Dream to do battle with dragons and evil men.

But it was Sancho Panza who made sure the horses got fed.

In 1491, a year before Columbus discovered the West Indies,
Inigo de Loyola was born in a Basque castle in the very country that Don Quixote and Sancho searched for giants. Inigo too
was to become a man unafraid to dream of a kingdom beyond
time and space, a kingdom burning beneath the surface of the
here and now. But he also knew that a starving man hears the
gurgle of his belly more clearly than he hears the voice of God.

Although they were of noble blood, the Loyolas were poor,
and so Inigo was never subjected to the deadening experience
of having too much money. However impoverished he was still

an aristocrat and by that very fact responsible for the people over whom destiny had set him. Like many another nobleman, Inigo was trained to exquisite courtesy and especially to a chivalrous attention to women. But courtesy will carry a man only so far, and there was not much hope that the eleventh of eleven children would prosper unless he entered the Church or lived by his wits and his sword.

For awhile he tried the Church. Inigo learned the basics of reading and writing. He was even tonsured. But inside him there boiled the spirit of adventure. He spelled his way through the heroic exploits of El Cid and Amadis of Gaul, men of delicate courtesy, honor, and truthfulness to be sure; but men who proved themselves more conclusively in battle and bedroom. Perhaps it is an ugly comparison, but the heroes of Arthurian legend were not unlike James Bond, hard fighting, hard losing, slightly tarnished heroes whose casual affairs of the bed only the heartless could refuse to forgive. This is what Inigo longed to be.

Obviously Inigo Loyola in a cassock was a tiger in a cage. A year before his father's death, when Inigo was sixteen, the boy was shipped off to be a page in the service of Juan Velasquez, Treasurer-General to King Ferdinand of Spain. It was a life too true to be good: tournaments with armored steeds, riding to the hunt, secret and tempestuous love affairs, arguments settled at sword's point. It was what he was born for.

Inigo was a courtier, a conquistador, a musketeer. The commandments were of course unquestionable in theory, but practice was entirely another matter. Church was for times of danger or for celebration of victory, and he never prayed so hard to our Lady as before a duel. In his last years when he had no need to be boastful, he was quoted by his secretary-biographer: "Though he was attached to the faith, he lived no way in conformity with it and did not avoid sin. Rather, he was much addicted to gambling and dissolute in his dealings with women, contentious and keen about using his sword."

Inigo found plenty of trouble. During carnival time, 1515, angered that his priest-brother had not been given charge of the church near Loyola (even though he had fathered children, apparently after his ordination), Inigo and some others of the clan managed to beat up some of the local clergy. When he was hauled into court, he tried to plead his clerical exemption from a civil trial, despite the fact that he had worn everything but clerical garb for years. Wisely he made tracks out of town.

But back-street brawling lacked the scope of his dreams, so in 1517 Inigo joined the command of the Duke of Najera occupying Pamplona on the border between France and the newly appropriated Spanish Navarre. The citizens of the occupied territory tolerated their new masters with fiery eyes. Their opportunity for revenge and freedom came when thousands of French troops poured through the passes of the Pyrenees to liberate them. Rejoicing villages greeted the French with open gates and the Council of Pamplona practically sent them the keys of the city. With more prudence than courage, the commander of the Pamplona garrison saw which way the wind was blowing and deserted. The hotheaded Inigo was furious and rallied around him the men willing to defend at least the citadel in the center of the town. When the captains actually saw twelve thousand men and thirty cannon drawn up against the city, it took all of Inigo's badgering and shaming to stiffen their backs to salvage, if not Pamplona, at least their own honor.

Father Bangert tells the story well: "The French offered terms of surrender. Ignatius persuaded the governor not to accept them. Because no priest was present, Ignatius, following a custom of the Middle Ages, confessed his sins to a comrade. Then he took his post on the breastworks. For six hours the French pounded the citadel, and finally part of the wall crumbled and the infantry prepared to pour in. In the breach stood Ignatius, sword drawn to meet the attack. And there he fell, his right leg shattered by a shell. Surrender of the garrison followed immediately.

"The French treated their wounded prisoner with that delicate courtesy which prompted them to carry him in a litter to Loyola, but which could never be a substitute for surgical

11

competence, so distressingly wanting when they tried to set
his broken leg. At Loyola the doctors of Azpeitia tried to remedy the mistakes of the French. It was an agonizing experience,
and years later Ignatius spoke of it as 'butchery.' He failed to
rally after the operation, became more and more weak, received the last sacraments, and almost died. Then came a turn
for the better and his strength gradually returned. However, the
doctors had left his leg in a condition intolerable to a man who
would still be the gallant courtier and soldier. The sections of
the broken bone did not mesh smoothly and evenly, one piece
actually resting astride the other. This caused a noticeable
protrusion and made the leg shorter than the other. Ignatius
could not abide this deformity and insisted on another operation,
even though it entailed agony of the worst kind. "

He bore it all in silence, he says, not for the love of God,
nor to do penance for his sins, but in order to wear again the
handsome tight-fitting boots which caught ladies' eyes.

As he lay at Loyola recovering from this second operation,
he whiled away the time with daydreams of his lady, a woman
he said was "more than a countess or a duchess." Whether
she was merely a creature of his hope and imagination or
Germaine de Foix, King Ferdinand's widow, he doesn't say;
but he spent hours and hours daydreaming of what he would
say to her, of the glorious deeds he would offer her as her
knight.

As the days dragged by, Inigo asked for books of chivalry
to feed his dreams, but all the castle could offer was The Life
of Christ and The Lives of the Saints, thin fare for one who
fed on battle and jousts and similar excitement. But when one
is lying alone for months in a sickbed, the silence begins to
scream, so he reluctantly picked up the two books. Without
his even suspecting, he was playing with fire, because these
two unappetizing books were going to eat away all those dreams.
He was moving into his first retreat.

Slowly turning the pages, Inigo found himself daydreaming about the lives of Jesus and the saints in the same way he
had dreamed away the hours with his princess. His curiosity

was caught by the fact that the book of saints called these men
"the Knights of God dedicated to the eternal prince, Jesus
Christ." They were men who drew from the gospels the courage to battle an evil more subtle than guns. He imagined himself as Dominic preaching and Francis begging; he saw himself walking the hills with Jesus. And his daydreams grew
overwhelming.

As John Kelly puts it, "He was meditating for the first
time on eternal truths, and his meditations--crude and un-
subtle as they were--would pull down his dream world and all
his castles in Spain about his ears. He was on the way to becoming the most painful and satisfactory thing a man can be-
come--a realist."

But then it began to fade. Gradually these thoughts yielded
to the old familiar glories in the gunsmoke, sabers flashing,
wounds borne proudly for the glory of the king. Then back
again to the yearning for a more elusive glory, binding wounds,
serving the poor, following a king from beyond time. As he
watched the swing of his thoughts, back and forth, he began
to see that his romantic daydreams left him empty and dry,
while his dreams of laboring with Christ gave him a profound
joy and peace. He began to suspect that the peace and joy he
felt was a touchstone of the truth, a call which said, more
and more certainly, that the glorious world of the court and
camp was less real and less permanent than the sacrificial
world of the cross. It was for him, as for all good men, a
disquieting suspicion.

He had come to that moment in every vocation when a man
stands helplessly before the Lord and asks, "All right! What
do you want me to do?"

Then one night as he lay awake, he, who to the end of his
life distrusted extraordinary phenomena, beheld very clearly the Blessed Virgin Mary holding the child Jesus. It was
a presence which threw his past, especially his sexual self-
indulgence, into a light from which there was no hiding. It
was the undeniable moment. He knew beyond doubt that he
was called to do battle not with temporary enemies but with

eternal ones: ignorance, greed, lust, all the manners of man's inhumanity to himself. He was a knight who had found his Lady and his King.

Ignatius was a great-souled, ambitious man, too big to live the comfortable quiet life of a kindly Christian. Once he chose a road, he went down it like a hurricane. Before the end of his convalescence, he had resolved to give up everything, to make a vow of perpetual chastity, and to go to the Holy Land. As sinner or saint, he could never be content to go halfway.

As he traveled toward the port of Barcelona, he stopped at the Benedictine shrine perched high in the mountains of Montserrat. After three days' preparing it in writing, he made a general confession. On March 24, 1522 with his past behind him, he began a completely new life. He gave his mule to the monastery, exchanged clothes with a passing beggar, hung his sword and dagger on the grill of Our Lady's chapel, and kept vigil there through the night in preparation for the new kind of battle he knew was about to begin.

There are writers who picture Ignatius Loyola as a cold soldier, grimly marshaling unquestioning automatons into battle. If they can look at this quixotic little man, kneeling through the night in his tatters before the Black Madonna of Montserrat and still call him a martinet, they are men who do not know the difference between a soldier and a knight.

The New Battle

There was much Ignatius had to discover about himself and about this new life he had been drawn into; and so, postponing his pilgrimage to the Holy Land, he remained at the little town of Manresa near Montserrat to wrestle with himself and with God. There, typically, he resolved to rival even the saints in his rejection of his past worldliness. As he says clearly in his meditation on the three classes of men, the worldly man is called to throw away everything, to free himself utterly from everything he is and has and claims: goods, clothes, position, friends, preconceptions, anything that might prevent him from seeing the world and himself and the will of God as they really are. Only then can he work back to what is essential for his true self in the hands of his King.

Because he had been so fastidious about his appearance, he now tramped through the village begging his food, body unwashed, hair and nails uncut, followed by a gaggle of urchins yelling after him, "Old bag! Old bag!" He helped the sick in the hospitals, attended daily Mass, and spent seven hours a day in prayer, on his knees.

Much later in his life, he says in his autobiography, "In those days, God was dealing with him as a teacher deals with a schoolboy . . . because he had no one else to teach him." But his teacher surely allowed him to make almost every possible mistake before correcting him. "By making mistakes, I learned not to make mistakes."

His penances were merciless. At first to copy the saints and then to prove his good will to God, he beat himself with a rope, fasted, slept rough and little. In the beginning it gave him great joy. It seemed so obviously the right thing to do, to teach the flesh who was in charge, to punish the instrument of his sins. It was much easier than discovering what he learned later, the slow crucifixion of unequivocal honesty about oneself. And then there were the temptations: It seemed cowardly and ungenerous to ease up on the penances. Yet to push them further was to court vanity for being so holy. But worst of all were the voices all beginners hear in their souls: "How can you possibly endure such a life for the seventy years you still have to live?" Even in his abandonment he was wise enough to answer, "You wretch, can you promise me even one hour of life?"

It was the dark night of the soul. Prayer became bleak torment; scruples over possibly unconfessed sins ravaged him. It was a nightmare so awful that he was tempted to suicide. Still continuing his regimen of prayer and penance, he resolved

"that he would neither eat nor drink until God came to his rescue . . . and all that week he put nothing in his mouth. "
And the scruples continued.

Then came the day of decision, palpable onslaught of grace, as if his teacher had finally taken him by the shoulders and shaken him. He resolved at that moment, once and for all, that he would never again confess his past sins. And he was, from that moment, unconditionally free.

Then, in a way most of us cannot even imagine, the soul of Ignatius opened to share in the aliveness of God. The most incandescent of these experiences occurred while he was sitting one day on the bank of the river Cardoner. Without seeing any vision, wave after wave of understanding enraptured him, filling him with a union of mind and will with God. It was an experience so intense that "he seemed to himself to be another man, with another mind than that which was his before. "

From that time onward he opened up more to people and took slightly greater pains to make himself agreeable to them. For this reason, after he had finally collapsed from his excessive fasting and penance, he cheerfully left behind him his more rigorous self-torments along with his outlandish clothes, his long hair, his long nails. It was not much, but it was a great advance on the sackcloth and a great advance in his spiritual growth.

The Spiritual Exercises

During this crucial period of his life, Ignatius began to sketch the lines of a little book by which others could attain the insights and freedom he had achieved without repeating his near-fatal mistakes. He envisioned a retreatant and his director working step-by-step through four weeks of meditations and contemplations in order to bring the retreatant to a freedom of vision where he could see God's will without his own fears or selfishness getting in the way.

Its basic premise, repeated over and over, is that growth in aliveness of the spirit is made only in proportion to the surrender of self-centeredness; there is only one Center. Over four weeks the retreatant ponders the purpose and fulfillment of human life and the sin which prevents it. He ponders Christ living human life to its fullest, loving his brothers even to the ultimate sacrifice of himself. He ponders Christ's sacrifice of himself leading to the resurrection of a new man born free of time and space, free of selfishness and death, free to love.

Every Jesuit described in the pages which follow made the thirty-day long retreat in his noviceship, before his first vows. If any one factor is common bedrock to every Jesuit, it is the union of vision and practicality embodied in the Spiritual Exercises of Ignatius Loyola.

No matter how different their lives were on the surface, each Jesuit based his life and work on the same principle and foundation: man was created to praise and serve God and by this means to save his soul, and in serving God man uses all the other things on the face of the earth, sickness or health, wealth or poverty, honor or dishonor, insofar as they help toward the goal and he avoids them insofar as they hinder it. With serene freedom he is to follow the paradoxical King, poor, generous, and loving, out into the world to spread the good news of the kingdom that has come.

It can be summed up in the sentence Ignatius spoke to his men going to the missions: "Go and set the world on fire!"

The Spiritual Exercises are the core of Jesuit training; and, along with its educational enterprises, they are the chief instrument of the Society's mission in the Church. But describing them to someone who has not made them is as inadequate as describing to someone who has never experienced it the liberating servitude of falling in love.

The Pilgrim

Toward the end of February 1523 Ignatius left Manresa for the Holy Land blissfully indifferent to the fact that he hadn't a single peso to his name. God wanted him to go to Palestine, and neither hell nor foul weather nor pirates nor Turks nor starvation was going to stop him. And on the way they all had a try at him.

But for nineteen memorable days he trudged from Holy Sepulcher to river Jordan, from Bethlehem to the Mount of Olives. Father Brodrick called him "this colossal tramp." With an idealism and determination one begins to expect, Ignatius made up his mind to stay in the Holy Land the rest of his days and convert the Turks. But the Franciscan superior there, fearing what a newly converted fanatic could do to uneasy relations with the Moslems, vetoed his plan in no uncertain terms. This was enough for Ignatius. If working in the Holy Land was his plan and not God's, he'd work elsewhere. So he boarded a a ship at Joppa for a three-month voyage back to Europe.

Ever since Manresa Ignatius had felt a restless need to help other men and women fulfill their lives. Since the Holy Land was behind him, he focused his enthusiasm on a resolution to study for the priesthood, a pilgrimage less dramatic than his trip to the Mideast but far more taxing. It was to be a journey of ten years.

Ignatius could already read and write, no small achievement for a nobleman of that time. Less than five percent of the adults at that time had an education equivalent to that of a seven-year-old today. But Ignatius knew no Latin. So at the age of thirty-three, the ex-caballero buckled his knees under desks alongside little boys and laboriously ground out Latin declensions for two years. Along with Saul of Tarsus and Augustine of Hippo, Ignatius of Loyola was definitely a delayed vocation.

From Barcelona he went to the universities of Alcala, Salamanca, and Paris. He begged his food, spent hours in prayer, and taught others to pray. He preached and discussed the Christian life. He was hauled in and out of jails as the Inquisition tested his teaching and found it orthodox. And all the while he was learning, even by making mistakes.

For instance at Alcala students could begin their studies at any stage they wished and were free to attend any lectures and take any courses they wanted. So Ignatius, a man in a hurry, took everything at once: scripture, literature, theology, and philosophy. After a year's work, he had nothing but a skullful of undigested ideas.

Ignatius also came to realize that although man does not live by bread alone, neither can he live without it. And yet if he spent long hours begging for tuition and food, he had no time to study or to pray. So he devised a schedule whereby he spent his summer vacations each year begging enough alms for the following term.

Although he was able to complete his master's degree in philosophy at Paris at age forty-three, theology ultimately defeated him. His earlier penances and his unremitting activity decisively broke his health so that he was never able to complete his theological studies for the doctorate. He tells us in his autobiography: "At this time in Paris, he was suffering a great deal from his stomach. Every two weeks he was in agony for a full hour, and this brought on a fever. On one occasion, the pain lasted sixteen or seventeen hours continuously. By the time he was finished his course of arts and was studying theology, the malady became progressively worse, and he could find no relief for it, though he tried many remedies."

For thirty years until his death Ignatius suffered this way. After embalming his body, the doctor wrote: "I extracted with my own hands almost numberless stones of various colors found in the kidneys, the lungs, the liver and the portal vein."

The bitter results of his uncritical enthusiasm gave birth to a realistic wisdom which still saves thousands of men trained in his Society from the same excesses: The course of a Jesuit's studies must progress step-by-step from grammar through theology. The main task for Jesuit students is to study

--other men can beg for them. A primary responsibility of every superior is to insure that no Jesuit is allowed to study or even to pray so much that his health is damaged.

"By making mistakes, I learned not to make mistakes."

The Society of Jesus

During these ten years of study Ignatius gave the Spiritual Exercises to a number of his fellow students. The first was his tutor and roommate in Paris, Pierre Favre, who confided in the older man the anguish of his scruples, his temptations, and the confusion he felt over what to do with his life. He was within months of priesthood but couldn't be sure it was the right step. He had come to an expert, and after a month making the Exercises with Ignatius, Favre was ordained a priest in May 1534.

Favre's other roommate, Francis Xavier,was another matter entirely. He was the youngest son of an impoverished nobleman who had died when Francis was still a child. Xavier had an iron determination to repair the damage to his family's fortunes. He didn't like Ignatius. The man who had moved in on them was fifteen years older, seedy, always sneaking in pious talk, and criticizing Xavier's inability to hang onto his money. What was worse, the man actually begged in the streets!

As Xavier's students began to grow in number and friends tactfully slipped him gifts to tide him over, he began to feel that his fortunes were on the rise. Then he found that both the students and the money had been sent indirectly by the cripple who panhandled in the streets. Finally, Francis began to be perplexed, to wonder, to soften, and, in the end, he made the Exercises. Instead of being a wealthy patron Xavier was to become the patron of missionaries. Ignatius himself said that Xavier was the toughest dough he ever had to knead. But Ignatius with his mind made up was a formidable kneader.

There were other men who made the Exercises too, but they later proved to be more focused on their own enthusiasm than on seeking the will of God, and Ignatius wished them well. But seven proved unshakable: Ignatius, Favre, Xavier, Simon Rodriguez, Diego Laynez, Alonso Salmeron, and Nicholas Bobadilla. Hour after hour they debated what God wanted of them with no idea that they might be making history.

Finally they decided to take three vows, poverty, chastity, and a pilgrimage to Jerusalem. If the pilgrimage were to prove impossible, they would go to Rome and offer themselves to the pope for . . . whatever. On the feast of the Assumption 1534 they left the Latin Quarter of Paris in the morning and Pierre Favre, their only priest, said Mass for them in the crypt chapel of St. Denis on Montmartre. At the Communion he turned with the host in his hands and each one in turn pronounced his vows. It was a moment of "unspeakable wonder" which none of them was ever to forget.

During the following months, through Favre's direction of the Exercises, three more joined the little company, Claude le Jay, Paschase Broet, and Jean Cordure. Now ten, they traveled to Venice to wait for a ship to the Holy Land and the blessing of the Holy Father on their pilgrimage. As the months passed by, one by one they were all ordained priests. But as wars around the Mediterranean postponed their passage again and again, the wait stretched out for two and a half years. They were not, however, sitting on the dock looking out to sea. By twos, they fanned out around the Italian countryside preaching, hearing confessions, giving the Exercises, working in hospitals, lecturing in scripture and theology, sheltering and feeding victims of the plague. Their reputation grew so rapidly that the pope called on them to settle disputes and take on the reform of monasteries.

Finally, as the will of God regarding Jerusalem gradually became obvious, the group met to decide their future. Should they preserve their union by taking a vow of obedience to one of their number who would keep them together and supervise the training of the new men? Or would that union shackle the freedom and mobility which was their greatest value? After weeks of talk and prayer, they decided to petition the pope to let them become a religious order, but with strong differences. The group would be primarily apostolic, not secluded in a monastery but out in the streets serving God by serving men. They would take a separate vow to go anywhere the pope chose, singly or all together. By their vow of poverty they would give up any right to own property, and they would refuse all offers of honor such as becoming bishops or cardinals unless express- ly commanded by the pope. Rather than participative decision making by elected chapters, the general's word would be final in any dispute. Finally, to preserve flexibility, they would not chant the Divine Office in common as all other religious com- munities did.

Rome moves like the tortoise and the snail. For another year of suspense they waited. But when Ignatius was convinced he knew God's will, he was unstoppable. To counter the objections of some cardinals, especially to the omission of singing the Of- fice, the ten Jesuits who were priests offered three hundred Masses apiece to soften the curial hearts. They sought letters from anyone of influence who had seen their work in Lisbon, in Ferrara, Parma, Bologna, Siena. At last on September 27, 1540 Pope Paul III made the Society of Jesus a reality with the bull Regimini Militantis Ecclesiae.

During the Lent of the following year, over his agonized protests, Ignatius Loyola at the age of fifty was unanimously elected the first general of the Society of Jesus.

The Early Years

In 1540 there were ten Jesuits. Sixteen years later when Ignatius died there were a thousand.

Like Johnny Appleseed, the Jesuits seemed to be everywhere at once stirring life wherever they went and rousing the inter- est of young men across Europe to become Jesuits. Broet was off to Siena giving retreats to university students. Le Jay set- tled a feud in Bognorea. Bobadilla went to Ischia; Salmeron and Broet to Ireland; Favre and Le Jay to Germany. Laynez and

Salmeron became most influential experts at the Council of Trent.

They were everywhere. Spreading aliveness. And they were busy. Le Jay wrote, "At present, I cannot get away from the church until midnight. On some mornings I find that they have scaled the walls and are actually settled inside my house waiting to go to confession. "

For the last four hundred years Jesuits have hardly unpacked their suitcases in any new field before they've started a school. Somebody once said that if two of them arrive in a new town in the morning, one of them has founded a high school by noon and the other has a college going before dark. And then they both teach in the night school after dinner.

It wasn't always that way. At first Ignatius feared schools because buildings tied men down. But he gradually came to see that if you want to set the world on fire, you have to begin with youth who are still pliable, before they are tempted to settle for a comfortable mediocrity.

From the very beginning of course, education in the sense of preaching and teaching Christian doctrine had been a part of the Society. But it had been a hit-and-run operation, two weeks here, three months there. Now, as the vocations flowed in, there was a large number of men whose studies forced them to stay a long while in one place. Within the first four years, Ignatius had set up residences in seven university towns so that the scholastics could attend classes. But Ignatius, whose own educational experience had taught him as much about the learning process itself as about books, wanted a place which would respect the different capacities of individuals and would lead each one at his own pace from literature through theology.

Consequently in 1545 Francis Borgia set up a college at Gandia in Spain exclusively for the training of Jesuits. Its reputation ran like wildfire and lay students begged to be allowed to attend the same classes. Ignatius agreed. It was a momentous decision. Within eight years the Society was running thirty-three schools. Today a third of all Jesuits are teachers. They run four thousand schools with a total of one million students.

The second major work of the Society, which actually began even before it was a religious order, was service in the foreign missions. As we will see over and over in the following pages, men branched out across the globe heedless of poverty, tempests, strange languages, and even treacherous Catholics. They vowed to go anywhere God called, and that call seemed everywhere. Within the first sixteen years there were Jesuits in India, Japan, the East Indies, Brazil, the Congo, and Ethiopia. Today, there are seven thousand Jesuits in missionary stations all over the world.

The General

Ignatius had been elected general against his will. For fifty years he had been on the move as a soldier, a pilgrim, an apostle. Even as a student he had been a beggar and a preacher. Uprootedness had been his natural state for half a century. But for the last sixteen years of his life because someone had to do it and because God had clearly chosen him for the job, the old fire-eater sat at a desk.

In those sixteen years he wrote six thousand letters, screened all applicants to the Society, opened homes for orphans and reformed prostitutes, but most important he carved out and fought for the Constitutions of the Society of Jesus. This document focused all the idealism of the Exercises into concrete activities and policies for admission, expulsion, intellectual and spiritual formation, the structure of the Order, the union among the members. And in all this he struggled to avoid the sterile rigidity that rule books invariably encourage. The Order had to be adaptable to any country or century. And so throughout the Constitutions is the constant refrain "according to what the intention of the Holy Spirit will suggest" and "always considering differing persons, places and times" and "according to what seems expedient." To Oliver Manare he wrote, "Man gives the orders, but God alone gives discernment. In the future I want you to act without scruple, according to what you judge the circumstances require, without regard to rules and prescriptions. " Concerning the Exercises he wrote, "There is no error more pernicious among masters of the spiritual life than desiring to govern others by themselves, thinking that what is good for them is good for all. "

The Constitutions were written to organize a group of men as prayerful as monks, as shrewd as pawnbrokers, and as different from one another as lions and lambs. The core of that unlikely union is, as in the Exercises and the Gospels, surrender of self for others. The Jesuit finds his own sanctification precisely in his self-forgetful work for the sanctification of everyone else. Even poverty, chastity, and obedience are primarily for others, to free the Jesuit to help. The conquest of self-centeredness aims at making the self a more flexible instrument in God's care for his children.

It took some screening to separate such unusual men from the novelty seekers, the escapists, and the self-improvers. At first Ignatius accepted anyone who showed up. But again by making mistakes he learned that "If there is one thing that makes me want to live longer, it is to be able to make it more difficult for candidates to enter the Society. " His chief test was whether a man could accept the scorn of the world and the poverty of Christ without losing his own conviction and joy. If the man was not yet that heroic, Ignatius asked if at least he had the desire to achieve that spirit.

By 1556 the sickness which had plagued Ignatius for years became worse. He had fits of shivering and fever and he often couldn't get up for days at a time. He moved to the house of scholastics in Rome and seemed to rally a bit. But resting was not his style. He had said long before, "The workers of the Society should have only one foot touching the earth, the other always raised to begin a journey. " On July 31, 1556 between six and six-thirty in the morning the colossal tramp of Loyola began his last pilgrimage.

Conclusion

St. Ignatius is often pictured by men who know him very little as a stern man of iron will and their descriptions of him bristle with military metaphors. Nothing could be further from the truth. A story told by one of his novices, Pedro Ribadeneira, may serve as an example.

"Since our Father was not eloquent, but unskilled in speech, and especially since he had studied the Italian language but little, I though only a boy, admonished this holy old man that there were many mistakes in his speech, many things which should be corrected because he gave them Spanish rather than Italian forms. 'Good!' he said, 'take note if any mistakes occur and correct me.'

"So the next day I began to observe our Father while he spoke, and to note down in writing any foreign words, incorrect pronunciations, and so on, in order not to forget them. But when I saw that not one or other word but the whole sermon would have to be changed, I despaired of any improvement and stopped taking notes and told our Father what had happened. And he said, 'Well, Pedro, what shall we do for God?'

"This is all the more wonderful since at that time I was a boy of scarcely fourteen. . . . But I recall one day he concluded a sermon by saying, 'Amar a Dio, con todo el core, con toda l'anima, con toda la voluntad. . .' a mixture of Spanish and Italian, but saying it with such force and fervor that his face seemed to glow. And sinners flocked to confession.

But how did this reputedly humble soul so often manage to get his own way? I suspect it may have been a personality factor he shared with Pope John XXIII, another simple man who set another whirlwind loose in the Church. The humility-strength contradiction is only apparent. Radical unselfishness leaves a man utterly free inside, free of preconceived ideas, free of fear, free of the opinions of others. It leaves a man amazingly able to adapt to the unforeseen and amazingly alive to the call of God from whatever quarter that call might come.

Like the prophets of the Old Testament, like Jesus himself, Ignatius was the executor of a cause which took possession of his mind. What appears as obstinacy is more really a loyal obedience to the inspirations of a King whose choices are unquestioned because they are beyond question.

The legacy of Ignatius was not a gift but a challenge: to serve God with unrelenting freedom, even from oneself.

A Warning and a Confession

Many of the men I teach have at best a tolerance for history. They say that human nature has changed so much, even in the last ten years, that no one who lived before 1960 has anything to tell them. The names of Joe Namath and Jimi Hendrix have more meaning than the names of Alexander and Henry VIII. The saints named at Mass are as meaningless as listings in a telephone book.

If you are one of these people, I suspect it would be best to close these pages, or skip ahead, or forget the whole thing. Part of Jesuitness is the richness each man gains from sharing a common humanity, a common gospel, and a common heritage with great Jesuits of the past. They are our brothers.

It enriches my vocation too to know that while Inigo Loyola swaggered around the court of Ferdinand the Great, Martin Luther was hammering his ninety-five theses to a door in Wittenburg. While Inigo lay shattered at Pamplona, Magellan was circumnavigating the earth. Inigo visited the London of St.

Thomas More and lived his last years in the Rome of Copernicus, Palestrina, and Cellini. Somehow I grow a touch knowing that when Brother Nicholas Owen was dying in London,
Rembrandt was being born in Amsterdam; and while Matteo
Ricci marched into the courts of Peking, Miguel Cervantes lay
in a Spanish dungeon scratching out the pages of Don Quixote
de la Mancha.

Self-aggrandizing perhaps. Romantic, surely. But enriching.

The number of Jesuits cited in the pages which follow is
limited for several reasons. Some of the great Jesuits of the
past were highly specialized in their work and their achievements are not easily understood today. Peter Canisius, for
instance, worked in Germany for thirty years, a bulwark
against the spread of Lutheranism. He taught, preached,
founded colleges, and wrote the first book ever published by a
Jesuit. But we are no longer hammering the Lutherans, and to
most men today Canisius' theological probings are as gripping
as a course in the minuet.

Again, Stanislaus Kostka at thirteen walked from Warsaw
to Rome in order to become a Jesuit and Aloysius Gonzaga gave
up a princedom to do the same. But telling their full stories to
young men today is almost sure to be boring.

To be perfectly frank, the crucial factor in choosing the men
described in the following pages is very simple: I like them.
They combine the two indispensible elements of real men: sensitivity and guts. They are men I would be proud to have at my
back in a fight, in a debate, in a class, or at an excruciating
formal tea.

The lives pictured here are too brief to do the men justice.
I have included a bibliography of full-length treatments of each
man at the end of the book.

On the other hand, one needn't read all the short lives which
follow to get an idea of what being a Jesuit means. Even two
or three will give some sense of what it means to be a Jesuit.
What follows is a group of fascinating men who found and lived
a Jesuit vocation.

For a very short time, Francis Xavier served, badly, as St. Ignatius' secretary in Rome. It was rather like harnessing Pegasus to a plow.

His liberation came abruptly and is one more example of how God meddles with the lives of those he loves trapping them into greatness. In 1540 before the Society had been approved Nicholas Bobadilla was slated to sail from Portugal on a probing action into the mission possibilities in the Far East. When he suddenly fell seriously ill, a handful of Jesuits were scattered all over Europe. Ignatius himself was sick in bed. There was only one man left, Xavier. Ignatius called him in, told him the situation, and said simply, "This is your job." Francis answered with equal simplicity, "Right. Here I am."

Then and there, as if this new assignment halfway round the world was not more than a week's jaunt in the country, Xavier set to work patching an old pair of trousers and a rather pitiful cassock. It was a trip from which he would probably never return. The next day he was on his way.

Xavier left Rome in March of 1540 and bristled for a full year in Lisbon before the expedition got underway. The voyage itself, down the west coast of Africa, around the tip of Good Hope, and across the Indian Ocean took another year. For the first sixty consecutive days Francis was unremittingly seasick. On May 6, 1542 more than two years after Xavier had left Rome, the lumbering Santiago finally edged into Goa, capital of the Portuguese East Indies.

For the next two years Francis worked among the pearl divers of the Fishery Coast painfully translating into Tamil the prayers of the rosary. From village to village under a broiling sun with only a handful of rice and an occasional piece of fish in his belly, he crossed and recrossed the arid beaches ringing a bell trying to lure the children to hear the story of a God who himself had walked unheeded among strangers. Suddenly, with no warning at all and probably more to blackmail the Portuguese into protecting their hides than to have Jesus protecting their souls, the natives moved en masse into the Church. In one bewildering month Xavier baptized ten thousand persons.

For the following four years Xavier toured the East Indian islands in a quest for conversions and for places where priests could best be stationed: Malacca, Java, Malaya, the Moluccas, Moro. Everywhere he went he went "with laughter in his mouth," and his letters home, recopied and shared in the Jesuit houses of Europe, were doing even more in Spain and Portugal than he was doing in the Indies. One rector said that if all the requests to join Xavier could have been honored, it would have emptied every college in Europe.

Xavier was a man who loved easily and he was man enough to speak of it unashamedly in his letters: "I say nothing of my love for you. The Lord, the searcher of hearts, knows how dear you are to me," and "Entirely yours, without my being able ever to forget you." The years by himself were a gift to God, indeed.

It was on this four-year trip around the islands that Xavier first heard of the islands of Japan which the Portuguese had discovered only five years before. And he also heard the first whispers of the great hidden empire called China.

In Xavier burned the soul of a conquistador. Japan was a challenge. And yet it gave him pause. This was not the barren and illiterate shore of the Fishery Coast. This was a country with a thousand-year-old culture, a land of men who were educated, proud, courteous, and unpredictably ferocious. What would they think of a white man gibbering at them in a barbarous language they couldn't fathom? Their Buddhist religion preached an emptying of self, but to the point of inertia. Was he going to reverse a thousand years? Besides it was a journey of three thousand miles through pirate-infested seas. One out of every three ships went to the bottom attempting to get there.

So of course Francis decided to go.

"I have almost always before me," he wrote, "the words I often heard spoken by our Father Ignatius: the members of the

Society should always strive hard to overcome themselves, and free themselves from all those fears that kill in a man faith, hope and trust in God. . . . When in doubt, never change what the soul has arrived at in light and calm. "

On August 15, 1549, fifteen years after his first vows on Montmartre, Francis Xavier landed at Kagoshima. At first he could only communicate in charades or through an interpreter. But gradually as he began to fumble with the language, he understood more clearly than ever that this was a missionary experience no man had ever faced before. Others, he himself, had brought the message of Christ to "natives," ignorant, self-seeking, primitive people who had nothing to lose but a few idols. But Japan was a culture, a whole world of values and ideas which had evolved into a total way of life without the slightest notion of Christ.

He found learned men accustomed to discussing the purpose of life. They were men who delighted in new ideas, turning them over slowly, fascinated by their facets, like children with jewels. And for that very reason Japanese conversions came not by the thousands but one by one.

Once again Xavier became the apostle of trudging through snow and freezing streams, feet uncovered, swollen and bleeding. He was rebuffed, laughed at, ignored.

With Ignatian adaptability, Francis decided to change tactics. Sitting in tea shops or on street corners with small merchants and scribes had yielded nothing but frustration. All right. He would visit a prince, not as a battered ascetic but with a display of grandeur, dressed in silk robes and offering an elaborate array of presents: a clock, spectacles, a music box, and wine.

It worked. The prince was so impressed by the round-eyed visitor and his presents that he gave him an unused Buddhist pagoda for living quarters and visitors swarmed in the gardens buzzing over the strange doctrines from the West. In two months what was to become a typically Jesuit willingness to adapt had yielded five hundred converts, not rice Christians but intelligent men and women who understood what they were freely choosing. So fertile were the possibilities that Xavier returned to Goa for reinforcements.

But the dream which was gradually taking shape in the back corridors of his mind was China, a small universe of pagans walled off from Europe and from Christ. After infuriating promises and betrayals and months of delays, Xavier finally sailed for the uninviting little island of San Chian just six miles off the Chinese coast. It was a haven for Portuguese smugglers, far enough to escape the eyes of the Chinese police but close enough for their less scrupulous commercial brethren. It was these Chinese merchants Xavier tried to bribe into taking him across to the mainland since all Chinese ports were sealed against foreign ships. But one by one they politely refused since it meant their heads if they were discovered. One merchant agreed, then never showed up.

The summer chilled into October, and even though Xavier doubled and redoubled his offers, the Chinese held back. But Xavier kept raising the stakes. The storm season was coming on fast and all but two Portuguese ships had headed back to Goa. Every day Xavier stood staring in mute frustration across the narrow straits. He was tempted to take the last ship south but couldn't bear the thought that one merchant might be greedy enough to open China to the kingdom. He had no food left and precious little clothing. Finally he fell sick with a burning fever. He became delirious and then lost the power of speech altogether.

His Chinese companion describes his last days: "At noon on Thursday, he regained his senses but spoke only to call upon the Blessed Trinity. . . . I heard him again repeat the words 'Jesus, Son of David, have mercy on me.' . . . He continued until the night of Friday passed on towards the dawn of Saturday, when I could see that he was dying and put a lighted candle in his hand. Then, with the name of Jesus on his lips he rendered his soul to his Creator and Lord with great repose and quietude."

In the odd ways of Providence, one month before Xavier's death the gentle genius Matteo Ricci was born in Macerata in central Italy. Thirty years later, dressed in silk and carrying clocks, Ricci was welcomed as a Jesuit mandarin and missionary to the imperial court of Peking. "Paul plants, Apollos waters, but God gives the increase."

In 1638, eighty-six years after Xavier's death, Japan closed her gates to foreigners and tried to eradicate the Church. There were three hundred thousand Catholics there then. In the purge which followed forty thousand of them went to martyrdom by decapitation or crucifixion rather than deny the faith, probably the largest group of martyrs in the history of the Church. Of the one hundred Jesuit martyrs in the Society's history, forty-four were Japanese.

Father Brodrick sums up Xavier well. "God be praised for great men's delusions, for where would the world be without them? Columbus suffered from them and Magellan and Galileo and Newton. And so too, did St. Paul, whose China was Spain. A man's reach should exceed his grasp, or what's a Heaven for? 'Delusions' is not the right word at all, but 'dreams,' and the dreams of Francis, as the subsequent history of Japan and China proved, had a way of becoming startlingly true."

St. Edmund Campion; 1540-1581   *Underground Jesuit*

Had Mistress Anne Boleyn been less calculating, she might have kept her head. As it was she kept her favors from King Henry VIII till he divorced his wife and made the young gamine his queen. Henry was a man long used to having what he wanted, so to get his divorce he was willing to wrest the power of the Church in England from the pope of Rome. And many an English martyr paid his life's blood for Mistress Boleyn's short-lived crown.

Thirty years after Anne was beheaded, her daughter Queen Elizabeth I paid a royal visit to the colleges of Oxford. Although the Church of England was a mere thirty years old, taking the Oath of Supremacy to the queen as head of the Church was already presumed by most scholars and hardly worth a second thought.

To celebrate the royal visit and to show off its faculty and students, Oxford prepared a week of speeches and debates for the scholarly queen, her secretary, Sir William Cecil, and her favorite, the Duke of Leicester. Like all administrators, Elizabeth was constantly in search of new talent to whom she could entrust the burgeoning business of what had become a worldwide empire. Her keen eye and ear singled out one speaker who interested her very much, Edmund Campion. At twenty-six he was only seven years younger than the queen herself. She sent Leicester to inform him, "Ask what you like for the present; the queen will provide for your future." Events were to prove that promise ironic indeed.

We have all known and envied men like Edmund Campion. This royal favor was just one more added to many already received. At seventeen he had come to Oxford and immediately attracted around him a group of students over whom he exerted an effortless influence. They crowded his lectures, imitated his speech, his mannerisms, his clothes.

And Campion knew how to play the game. He had no desire to embroil himself in disputes about the jurisdictions of Rome and Canterbury. Better men than he had taken the Oath, and if he could remain in the Established Church with a clear conscience, so be it. When receiving his master's degree in 1564, he took the Oath of Supremacy. He was ordained an Anglican deacon in 1568. He had everything a man could ask for, brilliance, popularity, and now an unavoidably rich and influential future.

By the statutes of the college Campion was obliged to proceed to the study of theology and to holy orders if he was to remain at Oxford. So he began his studies. But as he read through the Fathers of the Church, his security was undermined more and more. Was it possible that the truth about the Catholic Church had lain hidden for fifteen centuries and only recently had been revealed to a lusty young king and a caucus of nobles? On the other hand, Edmund's personal future was in the hands of this new church, which beckoned with titles of honor still to be won from an interested monarch. Campion made no secret of his unsureness and he buttonholed every man of knowledge who might put his misgivings to rest.

But Cecil's laws were making indecision less and less possible. There was no more time for continuing search. One was forced to either accept or rebel. Campion had three alternatives: to take the Oath of Supremacy at the hazard of his integrity and his soul; to make a clean break and join the Catholic expatriates on the French coast; or to buy time by accepting a post at the Irish University in Dublin.

Like Jonah before him, he fled his destiny by running in the opposite direction. On August 1, 1569 he took up residence in Dublin. But not for long.

Within six months of his arrival, Cecil instructed the authorities in Dublin to arrest even remotely suspected Catholics, and Edmund Campion packed up his books and his doubts and became a fugitive, a role he was to play for most of the rest of his life.

As he passed through London on his way to France, he witnessed the trial of Dr. John Storey, a Catholic refugee whom Cecil had kidnapped in Antwerp and brought home to face a mock trial for treason. The injustice of the trial and the ferocity of the sentence brought Campion's wavering to an end.

At Douai he made his confession, was received back into the Roman Church, and began two years of study for the priesthood while teaching rhetoric to his fellow seminarians. Douai was founded by Father William Allen in 1568 as a training center for underground priests. A more motley crew would be hard to imagine: elderly ex-professors, raw converts, ill-trained old priests, bitter fanatics whose families had been executed, even spies sent over by Cecil to discover their plans and English hiding places. It was Allen's task to sift and assign, some to writing, some to lecturing, and some to certain martyrdom across the channel. Twenty priests a year went from Douai to England. During Elizabeth's reign one hundred sixty died on the scaffold. Their lives "so gallantly squandered" accomplished more in a few months than many men's lifetime ministries.

There was now no question in Campion's mind about his vocation. On January 21, 1573 he set out from the coast of Normandy to enter the Society of Jesus in Rome. He walked.

From his novitiate Campion was sent for six peaceful years to Prague in Austria where he prayed, taught, produced plays, and studied. In 1578 he was ordained a Jesuit priest. Then on December 5, 1579 he received a letter from Father Allen at Douai.

"Our harvest is already great in England; ordinary laborers are not enough; more practiced men are wanted, but chiefly you and others of your order. The General has yielded to all our prayers; the Pope, the true father of our country, has consented; and God, in whose hands are the issues, has at last granted that our own Campion, with his extraordinary gifts of wisdom and grace, should be restored to us. "

On June 24, 1580 ten years after he had fled to the continent Edmund Campion landed at Dover in the guise of a jewel merchant. As he and his companions moved incognito from house to house in England, Catholics flocked to secret Masses. But how to tell the true believers? Were there spies in this congregation or weaklings willing to tell all under the slightest pressure? Almost from the time of his landing, Campion was pursued by agents of the crown.

"I ride about some piece of country every day. The harvest is wonderful great. . . . I cannot long escape the hands of the heretics. The enemy have so many eyes, so many tongues, so many scouts and crafts. I am in apparel very ridiculous even to myself; I often change it, and my name, too. "

Perhaps his most famous letter was a declaration of his intentions addressed to "The Right Honourable Lords of Her Majestie's Privy Council. " Copied from cell to cell in Marshalsea Prison, it spread like yeast through the English countryside. "Be it known to you that we have made a league--all the Jesuits in the world, whose succession and multitude must overreach all the practices of England--cheerfully to carry the cross you lay upon us, and never to despair your recovery while we have a man left to enjoy your Tyburn, or to be racked with your torments, or consumed with your prisons. The expense is reckoned, the enterprise is begun; it is of God, it cannot be withstood. So the faith was planted; so it must be restored. . . .

"I have no more to say but to recommend your case and mine to Almighty God, the Searcher of hearts, who sent His grace on us, and set us at accord before the day of payment, to the end we may at last be friends in heaven, when all injuries shall be forgotten. "

To the Council "Campion's Brag" meant conspiracy. To the Catholics it meant the revitalizing zeal of the Counter-Reformation. And for a full year Campion led the priest-hunters a merry chase.

All during the late spring he had been asked by a Catholic prisoner to stop and speak with his mother who lived with some nuns in Lyford. For a long time he had resisted since the house was already well supplied with priests and was notorious to the spies. But since he was passing so close, he stopped on July 11, 1581, said Mass, and departed. But the women couldn't contain their news; and as it spread, the Catholic neighbors felt cheated that they'd missed the experience of hearing the man who had refused the queen's promises, the man who could have been Archbishop of Canterbury. And the informers listened.

Meanwhile as Campion was in discussion with undergraduates in an Oxford pub, an unknown priest-hunter named George Eliot fell in with the group and begged Campion to return to Lyford for just one more Mass. Campion yielded. It was incautious, but he was wearying of the hide-and-seek.

On Sunday after receiving communion from Campion's hands, Eliot left Lyford in a rush to find the sheriff. When they heard the noise of the men surrounding the house, Campion and two other priests quickly hid behind a false wall. When the sheriff entered and the squire denied Eliot's accusations, the officer was caught between the word of a professional informer, rapist, and murderer, and the word of a member of the local gentry. He left.

But Eliot, with threats to report them directly to Cecil, forced the officers to return and for hours the men splintered the paneling to no avail. As night drew on the searchers went downstairs to sleep a few hours before beginning the search afresh. Deep into the night Campion came out of the hiding place to stretch his legs and encourage his terrified hosts. As he was getting back into the hole, someone stumbled. The guard was alarmed, but the priests got back into hiding without detection.

At daybreak, the search began again. Before noon the priests were discovered.

On the way back to London Campion's hands and feet were bound to his horse and a sign was pinned on the front of his hat saying "Campion the Seditious Jesuit." He was imprisoned in the Tower of London, questioned by Leicester, by Cecil, and, surprisingly, by the queen herself. They promised to forget the last ten years; he was too gifted a man to die. He refused to tell them anything.

For six months he was examined, stretched on the rack, cross-examined, racked, questioned by bishops and the queen's counselors, racked. At one trial he was so torn by the rack that he was unable to raise his right hand for the oath. One of the other prisoners kissed Campion's hand and raising it for him noticed there were no longer any fingernails on it.

Finally without the slightest shred of evidence he was condemned to death. When asked if he had any last words, he said, "In condemning us, you condemn all your own ancestors, all the ancient priests, bishops and kings, all that was once the glory of England. God lives; posterity will live; their judgment is not so liable as that of those who are now going to sentence us to death."

On December 1, 1581 he was dragged behind a horse through the mud from the Tower to Tyburn Hill and there he was hanged, cut down while he was still alive, and handed over to the butchers.

Persecution is not the worst thing that can happen to the Church. It brings back the spirit of the catacombs and winnows out the halfhearted. Those willing to risk their heads hearing Mass are not likely to yawn through it nor choose their priest because he gets the thing out of the way quickly. Each Mass is literally worth their lives. Persecution brings perspective.

During the time of the Elizabethan purge the Jesuits in England had a whole system of "safe houses" scattered across the island. They had set up a circuit of stops to serve the faithful along this string of stations. But this underground design had its hazards. People, even the best of people, find that a secret itches to be shared and there were enough men like George Eliot in England who were more than willing to share secrets with Lord William Cecil and his pursuivants.

At a word a hundred men could surround one of these "safe" houses, and if a priest were captured there, not only he but all those in the house would be imprisoned, tortured, and executed. The problem then was how to hide the priest; and the man who solved it was an architectural genius named Nicholas Owen, a Jesuit brother known as "Little John."

For sixteen years with his tool bag over his shoulder Little John tramped up the drives of country estates and would quote a price for patching a roof or repairing a floor. To the servants he was just another wandering tinker. But his real work was at night. While the house slept, Little John was at work on a cubbyhole, hacking through ceilings, burrowing below the bottoms of fireplaces and behind cupboards. No two hiding places were alike; the discovery of one could not lead to another.

Father John Gerard who owed his life many times over to Owen's craft writes, "At Baddesley Clinton he constructed a hiding hole in a sewer running the entire length of the back wing which could accommodate a dozen or more priests. The old discharge into the moat and the loopholes which lit the

tunnel had been camouflaged; and a garderobe turret, into which
the sewage was diverted, constructed to project from the wall.
The main entrance to it was down a shaft from a room adjoin-
ing the chapel. There was a second entrance from the room
used by the priests in residence. "

A scholar named Granville-Squiers made a study of secret
hiding places in old English manor houses. Of the crafty little Jesuit's hiding holes he says, "It is noticeable in Owen's
work that he nearly always contrived an emergency exit or
bolt-hole to his hideaways and whenever possible linked them
up so that one could be used in conjunction with another. He
was also fond of constructing one hiding place within another
and sometimes a third, so that if one were discovered, it
might be thought empty and left. The plan he followed whenever possible was to burrow under solid masonry, for a few
inches of brick or stonework with a plaster lining will give
out no hollow sound. "

Owen's provincial Father Henry Garnet wrote: "I verily
think no man can be said to have done more good for all those
that labored in the English vineyard. For, first, he was the
immediate occasion of saving many hundreds of persons, both
ecclesiastical and secular, and of the estates of these seculars,
which had been lost and forfeited many times over if the priests
had been taken in their houses. . . . How many priests, then,
may we think this man did save by his endeavors in the space
of seventeen years, having labored in all the shires and in
the chiefest houses of England?"

Little John walked with a limp. Years before he had had an
accident with a horse which left him partially crippled. The
limp was worsened by a rupture which he had gotten in the
heavy work which secrecy forced him to do alone. But he
never spoke of limp or rupture. He lived very much on his
own, and his greatest value besides his architectural skill
was that to the end he kept his mouth shut. So tight-lipped
was he that no one knew his age and, although he and Father
Gerard had traveled and worked together for years, had been
captured, imprisoned, and racked together, Gerard him-

41

self was never certain whether Owen was a Jesuit!

Surely Little John was a quiet man, but he had a fierce spirit of loyalty. He had wagered his life for Christ to save priests, great-hearted friends like Campion, Gerard, Garnet, Robert Persons, and Robert Southwell. So when Campion was so iniquitously tried and so barbarously executed, it is not difficult to understand how Little John's fury at the injustice could burst from him. From out of the crowd at the scaffold he shouted that Campion was an innocent man. He was arrested, tortured, and released without his captors realizing what a prize they were setting free.

In 1605 several Catholics with more courage than brains were apprehended in the Gunpowder Plot. This gallantly witless attempt to blow up Parliament served only to step up the search for priests. There were pictures of the Jesuit provincial everywhere in the streets so that he, Father Oldcorne, Brother Owen, and Brother Ashley slipped away to hide at Hinlip Manor until the worst of the furor died down. But the pursuivants were not to be outfoxed.

On Sunday morning January 21, 1606 a hundred searchers surrounded Hinlip. With the two priests cramped into one hiding place and the two brothers in another, the pursuivants first searched in the obvious places under beds and in cupboards and then began a six-day methodical movement from one room to another ripping out paneling and chimneys, measuring upstairs rooms against the size of the rooms immediately below. In the end hoping to satisfy the searchers with a catch that would send them away, the two brothers came out of hiding and by their evasive answers attempted to convince their captors that they were priests.

It didn't work, and the priests were soon discovered. Had they not been, it is likely that they would have died anyway, if not from hunger then from the stench of the hiding hole. Gerard reports that "the place was so close that those customs of nature which of necessity must be done . . . were exceeding offensive to the men. The priests confessed that they had not been able to hold out one whole day longer, but either they must have squealed or perished in that place. "

Owen's fate was inevitable since he carried in his head the secrets of so many hiding places which the government resolved to get out of him at any cost. A jubilant Cecil wrote, "It is incredible how great was the joy caused by the arrest throughout the kingdom, knowing the great skill of Owen in constructing hiding places and the innumerable quantity of these dark holes which he had schemed for hiding priests. . . . No dealing now with a lenient hand. We will try to get from him by coaxing, if he is willing thus to contract for his life, an excellent booty of priests. If he will not confess, he shall be pressed by exquisite tortures, and we will wring the secrets from him by the severity of his torments. "

Day after day, for seven hours a day, they fastened him by the arms to a beam and added more and more weights to his legs. Knowing Owen had a rupture, the torturers fastened iron straps around his body to insure the maximum of torture and prevent the possibility of premature death by natural causes. The little man merely repeated over and over, "Jesus. Mary. "

Finally, it was one more weight too many. The iron straps themselves burst and the brother's bowels gushed out with his life.

Cecil published a report that Little John had stolen a knife and, unguarded, committed suicide by disembowcling himself to escape further torture.

Many of his hiding places were discovered only when they were bombed during World War II. Many more still remain to be found. Some of them, like their remarkable builder, will hold their secrets forever.

Like many well-meaning fathers, Giovanbattista Ricci had
plans for his son before the boy was weaned. He himself had
moved up from being a simple pharmacist to being mayor of
his town. His oldest boy was going to study in Rome; he was
going to be a lawyer; he was going to make a real name for
himself. And his father? A governor, perhaps, or an advisor
to a prince. God and his son, however, had other plans; and
after three years of law school in Rome, Matteo Ricci knocked
on the door of the Jesuit novitiate. If he hadn't, history most
probably would never have heard of the Riccis, pere or fils.

During his regular Jesuit studies Matteo encountered a
very remarkable man, Father Christopher Calvius, the most
brilliant mathematician of his time. In the hands of this poly-
math, Ricci found mathematics all-engrossing and he moved
slowly from geometry to astronomy and gradually out into the
mesmerizing movement of the stars and then back to earth
to construct sundials, clocks, spheres, and astrolabes. Without realizing it Christopher Clavius was forging the key to
the heart of Cathay.

After repeated petitions, Matteo Ricci was finally appointed
to finish his seminary program in the missions of the Far
East. He taught at Goa and Cochin, completed his theology,
and in 1580 was ordained a priest.

At that time, as in the time of Francis Xavier, China was
still a dream, sealed off from both the good and bad influences
of the West. It was the most populous kingdom on earth, in-
dustrious and peaceful. Its government was in the hands of
philosophers wise and unwise enough to wall out foreign contamination.

But China was not totally altruistic. Trade promised so
much wealth both for Portugal and China that a precarious
compromise had to be reached. In 1557 the Portuguese were
permitted to lease Macao, part of a small peninsula in the
Canton Bay. The Chinese walled off the landward side and

guarded the gates night and day.

Alessandro Valignano, Xavier's successor as Jesuit superior, was shrewd enough to realize that the Portuguese traders were merely tolerated in Macao and would be expelled from China the instant they ceased to be useful. Valignano knew that if the Church were to gain a lasting foothold in China, it would have to free itself from the stigma of European commercialism and adapt itself as far as possible to local customs and beliefs. Only this way would the message of Christianity be intelligible, not to say acceptable to the Chinese.

From his experience in the Far East Valignano was convinced that China, which practiced religious toleration and admired learning, would be naturally disposed to Christianity. But previous missionaries entering the country and unable to speak the language were taken for Portuguese spies, arrested, and unceremoniously shipped back to Macao.

Therefore Valignano adopted a dramatic new plan. The Jesuit missionary must now do what no Westerner had ever attempted; he must learn to read, write, and speak Chinese as well or better than a mandarin. He must study the government, laws, religion, and science of China so well that the Chinese would not see him as a predatory foreigner but as a brother with knowledge to share.

Two years after his ordination in Cochin Matteo Ricci was summoned to be Valignano's spearhead into China.

He was the perfect choice. His untiring energy and prodigious memory enabled him to learn Chinese with remarkable speed. And Valignano hoped that his wide knowledge of natural science could lure the philosophic mandarins beyond physics and astronomy into discussions of philosophy and theology. In early September, 1583 disguised as a Buddhist monk at the invitation of the governor of Shiuking Matteo Ricci sailed in a sampan into the sealed empire of China. He was never to return.

Xavier's easement of poverty in favor of the kingdom had not been a lesson lost. When Ricci produced his rich presents for the governor, he became an instant celebrity. First he held up a prism of Venetian glass and a small painting of our Lady. The mandarins treated the objects like stars from heaven; they feared to look at them much less touch them. In an area of China where plain glass was unknown, the prism was a crystal which captured the rainbow. Ignorant of perspective in art, some of the onlookers around the painting fell to their knees and bowed to the ground in worship of this tiny, living lady.

As Ricci settled in, mandarins visited him more and more frequently to see his treasures. The most remarkable treasure was his map of the world with China in proper perspective. These learned men became more and more intrigued and the new wise man from the West began translating articles on mathematics and literature into Chinese. He also translated a few stories of the Lord of heaven. As the years passed and opportunities arose or the local situation became dangerous, Ricci gradually moved further and further north--Shiuchow, Nanchang, Nanking--always closer to the center of influence in China, Peking.

In 1594, after eleven years' apprenticeship in China, Ricci discarded his ragged grey Buddhist robes and donned the purple silk gown and the tall black mitre of the recognized mandarin. He was now Li-Matou.

Ricci had written the Jesuit headquarters in Macao that if he had been able and if it would have made the Chinese more susceptible to Christ, he would not only have surrendered his cassock but would have changed the shape of his eyes and the size of his nose too. His goal was not to multiply baptisms but to give Christianity an acceptable place in Chinese life. Without that it would always be at the mercy of capricious governors as it had been in Japan. His method was not through sermons but through conversations, and his new friends radiated his science and his Christianity throughout the provinces. He made the soil of China less and less hostile to the seed of the gospel.

He was not without his critics, even among his brothers at Macao and Goa. Not wearing his Jesuit cassock was bad enough, but what they considered his tolerance of ancestor worship was heresy pure and simple. Ricci replied that he was certain that the Chinese respect for Confucius was no more idolatrous than his respect for Aristotle. Their rituals for their ancestors were in fact no more religious than our laying a wreath at the tomb of the Unknown Soldier. But judgments are always easier at a distance.

At last in 1598 through the influence of his friends Ricci arrived in Peking. But because of a war with Japan in Korea (there is nothing new under the sun) and the continuing Chinese fear of spies and foreigners, even some of his long-time friends in the capital would not receive him. He began to run short of cash then and had to turn south again.

It had not been a total waste of time. He had seen the ways of politics in the capital, especially the power of the king's eunuchs. He and his companions had also worked out a phonetic method of writing Chinese in Roman characters and had calculated the latitudes of the cities to prepare an accurate map of China. From these studies Ricci was convinced that China was none other than Marco Polo's long-fabled land of Cathay--a theory later proved true in 1607 by the journeys of a Jesuit brother, Benito de Goes.

Back down in Nanking, Ricci set about solidifying his influences at the capital. Through his scholarship, his ability at map making, and especially his descriptions of charitable institutions in Europe unheard of in China, he became friends with the president of the Imperial Supreme Court and with the Ministers of Justice and Finance.

With their letters of introduction, he once again set out through the jungle of tax-collecting eunuchs on his way to Peking. On January 27, 1601 the palace eunuchs presented Ricci's gifts to the unseen emperor, a painting of the Madonna, a Roman breviary, two glass prisms, a spinet piano, and two clocks, the smaller of which was more valuable but the larger of which was more valued since it made more noise. Ricci sent a letter with his gifts stating that he was a foreigner drawn to China by its great name, a doctor of science who had spent fifteen years in the country. He was a monk without wife and children and therefore seeking no favor. But having studied astronomy, geography, calculus, and mathematics, he would be honored to be of service to his Imperial Majesty.

As in his first meeting with the Chinese, Ricci found the imperial court astonished by the prisms and the paintings, but the piece de resistance was the chiming clock. By luck or design it was a gift which kept running down, and in order to "fix" it Ricci was allowed to enter at least the outer precincts of the forbidden city. Every day a eunuch came to his quarters to learn how to keep the clock "alive" and another to learn how to play the spinet. It was at least a beginning, and Matteo Ricci with all his learning was wise enough to realize that he was only a beginning.

The legend has somehow persisted that Ricci was on intimate terms with the emperor. Actually he never saw him. The emperor spent all of his time in high seculsion with his concubines with the result that even when Ricci's first gifts were presented, the ambassador from the West bowed only to an empty throne. The rare times Ricci was allowed back into the palace were only to repair the clocks. But this was all he needed since no one could reside within the forbidden walls of Peking without at least tacit approval of the emperor. Therefore, at least for the moment, Christianity was safe.

Just as at Nanking, conversations filled his days so that sometimes he had no time to eat. "Without going out of the house we preach to the gentiles, some of whom are converted. As for the majority of our visitors, little by little through the contacts which they establish with us, God softens their hearts." Thus from the modest parlor of his residence his quiet voice and influence reached out to every part of the sprawling empire through the thousands of scholars who came to Peking for civil service examinations seeking influential positions but hungry for the truths of man's life.

Ricci's message was multiplied through his books. His little manual of Christian doctrine was reprinted again and again, and its appeal was enhanced by the reputation of the man who also translated Euclid's mathematics, Clavius' astronomy, and all sorts of other works from geography to hydraulics.

Not yet sixty and apparently in good health, Ricci had an uncanny foreboding of his impending death. At last worn out by crushing years of study and work and uncertainty, he received viaticum. And without much drama in a converted Buddhist pagoda the wise man from the West died.

Immediately after his death the prime minister of China secured the emperor's permission to declare him a Chinese citizen and to assign him a worthy burial ground. Ricci was not wrong in this premonition that his death too would serve the Church; for in recognizing the greatness of Li-Matou, the emperor also gave recognition to Li-Matou's religion. Over his grave was erected a monument engraved with the names of hundreds of mandarin scholars who revered his knowledge, his friendship, and even his teachings.

The first Christians in Peking were few but they were influential. Matteo Ricci baptized his first two Peking converts in 1601. In 1605 there was over a hundred. In 1609 the year before he died, there were four hundred. Fifty years later there were 150,000 Catholics in China. And eighty years after Ricci's death the Emperor K'ang-hsi promulgated an edict of toleration for the Christian religion.

Since then thousands of Jesuits have followed this genius into the gates of the hidden kingdom, and even now in the prisons of China Chinese priests and Chinese Catholics live in the same belief, the same trust that China will one day open its gates and its heart to the Good News.

St. Jean de Brebeuf, 1593-1649   *Giant to the Hurons*

In 1633 nine French Jesuits established a settlement for Algonquin Indians near Sillery in Quebec. But for most of the Jesuits this was only a preliminary headquarters. The Algonquins were willing to settle down to a farmer's life, but the Hurons were nomads moving on to more promising hunting grounds with the herds of game. If the gospel were to be preached to the Hurons, it would have to be brought by canoes down the St. Lawrence and along the shores of the Great Lakes. To reach the populous Hurons wherever they threw up their temporary villages, the Jesuits planned satellite stations across southern Canada. Each had a few priests living together who were able to fan out singly to the Huron villages around them.

In midsummer of 1633 Jean de Brebeuf and two other Jesuits set out with a group of Hurons for Georgian Bay, the great body of water which bellies out from the north side of Lake Huron. Brebeuf was a big man, six-foot-three, but the journey was still exhausting. He wrote, "We had to row from morning till night, and the only time we had to read our breviaries was at night by the light of the campfire. In the portages, that is where there are waterfalls, we had to transport our baggage by land, sometimes having to make as many as four journeys to and fro with burdens we could hardly carry."

At Ihonatiria on Georgian Bay Brebeuf began sixteen years of almost uninterrupted work. The first job was to set up a residence. The house was a primitive wood cabin with the bare earth for a table and bark plates and cups. Food was usually Indian sagamite, pounded corn boiled in water, which one Jesuit said "resembled nothing more than the paste used to paper walls." Beds were bundles of bark and branches piled on the bare ground. But one of the Jesuits with a knack for carpentry jury-rigged a few partitions and doors which the Indians found marvelously elegant. But that was about as far as their fascination went for the white man's ways.

Most people, Brebeuf's Indians or Ricci's mandarins or white-collar workers today, are more or less settled into the lives they lead. The revolutionary message of Christianity is something they would prefer to ignore, or if that's impossible, to dilute into a few pious practices where its call will cease to be threatening.

Therefore the most effective way to introduce the message of the gospel is to bring it in the back door. The apostle must earn the respect of his audience with some nonreligious activity that they do find valuable. This way his Christianity at least has a chance of getting a hearing.

This is why Ricci taught mathematics, why de Nobili taught the Vedic scriptures, why Jesuits today teach chemistry and put on plays and run for Congress. This is why Brebeuf offered his big shoulders and his strong back to paddle canoes with Huron hunting parties sometimes for months at a time to be with the people, to learn their susceptibilities, to earn their grudging respect, to soften their resistance to the message of Christ.

It was not an easy life. The native huts they stayed in were little more than sheds of bark and poles with long sleeping platforms for as many as twenty families. Not the slightest privacy. Fires burning constantly filled the hogans with smoke and left everyone with seared, reddened eyes. Waking or sleeping, the Jesuits were harassed by vermin, dogs, and scrofulous children. Marriages were temporary, thieving was commonplace, and the return of hunting parties meant orgies of gluttony. Worst of all was the torture and slaughter of prisoners of war which the missionaries were often obliged to witness helplessly. The victims were burned, mutilated, and finally devoured so that their strength would pass into the bodies of their executioners.

In 1640 as Brebeuf was returning from four months of fruitless effort with a tribe of Neutrals near Niagara Falls, he saw a huge cross in the sky coming from across the lake, the land of the Iroquois. When his brothers asked how large the cross had been, he answered, "Large enough for all of us."

It was a portent that was to come tragically true. In 1646 Isaac Jogues and Jean de la Lande were tomahawked to death at Auriesville, New York. In 1648 Anthony Daniel was butchered in the blazing ruins of his mission station. And 1649 would be the year of Lalement, Garnier, Chabanel. It would be the year of Jean de Brebeuf himself.

One night in March while the Jesuits were sleeping, the air around the mission suddenly erupted with war whoops and the Iroquois burst into the cabin with tomahawks and torches.

51

The Jesuits were dragged out into the clearing and their house was ransacked. As dawn began to break, their last agony began.

Brebeuf was hauled to his feet, stripped, tied to a post, and brutally beaten. Then in a mockery of baptisms he had seen, a renegade Huron poured boiling water over the big man's head and face. Others heated a collar of hatchets in the coals of the fire and strung them around his neck, pressing them against the flesh of his shoulders and chest. Two Indians tied a belt of bark and pitch around his naked waist and set it afire. But Brebeuf's refusal to cry out infuriated his tormentors and his continual prayers so enraged them that they tore out his tongue and ripped off his lips.

While he still sagged half-alive against the pole, they tore flesh from his thighs and roasted it and ate it while he looked on through his bleared and bloody eyes. Then they scalped him, and finally one of them, seeing that he was about to die, drove a knife into his chest, cut out his heart, and roasted it so that the Iroquois could devour it and ingest into themselves the courage of this giant.

His tortures began early in the morning. He did not die until four o'clock in the afternoon.

By the end of 1649 the Huron nation had been all but exterminated by the Iroquois, and the laboriously built Huron mission was abandoned for a time. But it proved to be "one of the triumphant failures that are commonplaces in the Church's history." The martyrdoms created a wave of vocations and a missionary fervor in France. What was more important, it paradoxically gave new heart to the men already in New France. Like the Iroquois, they had taken the courage of Brebeuf into themselves.

Nine years before his death Brebeuf had made a vow that martyrdom would not elude him. The vow ends with these words: "And since you have deigned to die for me, I therefore, my beloved Jesus, offer you from this day forth, in the sentiments of joy which I now feel, my body, my blood, and my life, in order that I may die for you alone. Let me so live that you will grant me this favor of dying thus happily. Therefore, my savior and

my God, I take from your hand the chalice of suffering and I
will invoke your name: Jesus, Jesus, Jesus. "
His savior took him at his word.

The Paraguay Reductions, 1610-1750   *Jesuit Welfare State*

The stories in this book have been, till now, the lives of individuals, men trained to communal living but most often
working alone. The Paraguay Reductions of the seventeenth
and eighteenth centuries were chiefly the work of an organized
group of Jesuits. It was a highly international group, Jesuits
from Spain, Italy, Germany, Flanders, England, and Ireland
who conducted an astonishingly successful experiment in peaceful and prosperous living in communities ranging over an area
as large as Texas.

The two main obstacles to the spread of Christianity among
the South American Indians had always been the nomadic habits of the natives and the brutality of the Spanish and Portuguese
merchants, slavers, and adventurers. In order to protect the
tribes the Jesuit provincial of Paraguay, Diego de Torres,
sailed directly to Spain and successfully petitioned King Philip
III for a royal edict outlawing Indian slavery. Then de Torres
and his men began to set up an Indian commonwealth in the
interior of South America. It was an ingenious, heroic, creative plan that worked far too well to last.

Unlike the Indians of North America, these natives were
naturally kind, trusting, cheerful--and lazy. When nature had
provided so abundantly for their simple needs, why stay in
one place and undertake the daily routine of agriculture? To
make such people think of the future was like teaching children to be frugal.

In 1609 Fathers Cataldino and Maceta began the first village with two hundred families of Christian Guarani Indians.
Despite their chafing over the settled life and regular work,
the Indians were gradually won over to a life where orgy and

starvation did not alternate like night and day. Even if they had to work, they were at least protected from the slave-hunting colonists.

The worst of these slavers were the mamelucos from Sao Paolo. They were half-breeds, runaway criminals, and deserters wandering the country looking for an easy life and native women. Slave trading provided both. For them the Reductions were reservoirs of slaves just over the border. Their greed overcame their hesitation and drove the slavers to hack their way through the jungles, to surprise whole villages where thousands of unarmed Indians were walking gold.

The attack was almost always the same, sudden and savage. The slavers surrounded the village, set the outbuildings afire, and with their muskets drove the panicked villagers into the central square. The natives were bound together in couples for the long trek to the slave market, but the old and sickly were simply tied together and thrown into the burning buildings. A royal edict might mean something in Spain, but hundreds of miles behind the green wall of the Paraguayan jungle it was merely a piece of paper.

The raids became so numerous and brutal that in 1630 alone about thirty thousand Indians were killed or enslaved.

In desperation the Jesuits undertook the enormous project of moving the entire population of ten villages to new sites deeper in the interior, away from the mamelucos. When the slavers still followed, Father Antonio Ruiz sailed to Madrid in 1637 and obtained permission to arm and train the Indians. This militia, trained by Spanish officers and some of the Jesuits who had been soldiers, put an end to the raids.

The streets of the Indian villages were laid out in a grid, like Manhattan or San Francisco, with six to ten one-story houses in a block; each house was divided into separate family apartments. In the center of the village was a tree-shaded plaza with the church, workshops, and a hospital. The village served anywhere from three hundred to ten thousand people who worked the farmlands around the village.

The Reductions worked like a system of cooperatives. Each family owned a piece of land, and there were trading centers in each village where they could barter for fabrics or jewelry or imported knives, scissors, or farm tools. Each village had workshops where the natives were trained in metallurgy, cattle raising, architecture, and printing. And the high Masses in the church were celebrated with a full choir and orchestral

The farms were worked collectively and food was rationed. Formerly an Indian with a whole side of beef would gorge his family for a night and then starve for weeks. The only trade beyond the village was with other Reductions. Strange white men could live in a village only on a pass and only for a very short time.

All was not idyllic, however. There were jails, and whipping for serious offenses, but no capital punishment. Some Indians rebelled, and in 1628 five of the Jesuits were murdered. For such grievous crimes the guilty were merely driven from the Reduction and forced to faced the mamelucos on their own.

Historian Denis Meadows has written, "The story of the events that wrote finis to the Paraguay Reductions is a compression of the white men's greed, heartless bureaucracy, vandalism, and man's inhumanity to man generally, crowned by the smug egotism of a stupid king. The desire of the European colonists to dispossess the Jesuits and seize their missions began with Spanish and Portuguese hatred of the Society for its opposition to Indian slavery and its enlistment of royal support for this policy."

The colonists' eagerness to take over the Reductions was also fueled by myths of gold mines and great wealth hidden in the villages. The mission books in fact show that most Reductions had difficulty breaking even each year.

In the middle of the eighteenth century the Portuguese made an agreement with the Spaniards to yield up the slave trading port of Sacramento along the Plate River which the Spanish had long wanted to clean out. In exchange the Portuguese were to receive the seven Reductions in the Uruguay region. By the treaty of 1750 the missionaries and their thirty thousand Christian Indians were ordered to abandon their homes, pack up, and get out.

The patience of the Indians broke. They had trusted Spain and loathed the Portuguese who to them meant only the mamelucos. They rebelled against the betrayal of their trust and, in a pitiable little war between two well-armed European armies and a horde of Indians with spears and a few muskets, the Indians were inevitably defeated.

The villages of the Uruguay region were deserted, the land reverted to jungle, the churches and towns moldered into ruin. And there was no gold.

This was, however, the cloud no bigger than a man's hand which appears on the horizon and gradually builds into a devastating storm. In 1767 there were fifty-seven Reductions with a population of 114,000 natives. But in that very year King Charles of Spain declared the expulsion of the Jesuits from all Spanish colonies. His reasons, he said, were reserved in his royal breast.

It was the beginning of the end. Six years later at the concerted behest of the Bourbon monarchs, the Jesuit Order was suppressed throughout the world.

The Suppression of the Jesuits, 1759-1814

St. Ignatius often said that the worst thing he could imagine being called on to face would be the dissolution of the Society; but he felt sure that if the pope, expressing the will of God, told him to dissolve the Society, he could do it, provided he had time for fifteen minutes of prayer.

Had he lived till the end of the eighteenth century, he would have had that burden.

It was a time not entirely unlike our own. The nations of Europe were gorged with the wealth of their new colonies and even men in the street were beginning to realize that Europe was the greatest "country" in the history of the world. The time was relatively peaceful with some saber rattling but a general feeling of detente. The rising middle class was making sure that its sons were being educated at least as well as young dukes. In the salons of France and Spain, men and women were no more moral than they had to be.

What was more important, however, was that this was the Age of Enlightenment--an era when man was the measure of all things, when reason could answer all questions if it were given time, when humanism, and the Bourbons, were king.

As Father William Bangert writes: "Exaggerated as it is to say that Europe in the 12th century had become one great Citeaux, this judgment nevertheless highlights the pervasive influence of the Cistercians. Again allowing for obvious overstatement, it might be said that between 1570 and 1760 the Catholic world had become one great Jesuit school. In neither case did the honored ascendency last. As the history of the Church unfolded, the developments of the 12th century Renaissance and the arrival of the friars terminated what have been called the Benedictine centuries. In the late 18th century the Enlightenment closed what can be appropriately called the Jesuit centuries."

The Age of Enlightenment brought in an era of cynicism epitomized in Voltaire, a former Jesuit student. In 1722 the Duchess of Orleans wrote that she did not think there were a hundred people in all of Paris, clerics as well as laymen, who believed in Christ. And Voltaire wrote, "Once we have destroyed the Jesuits, we shall hold a good hand against the detestable Thing (the Church)."

Behind the hostility of the Philosophers was an honest search for justice, truth, and human dignity; but the Society at the time had no theologian of the stature of Bellarmine to join them in their search and, like Ricci, harmonize the truths of the gospels and the truths of the Philosophers. These men had a just grievance against the stagnant, nit-picking scholasticism of many Jesuit texts and courses. Somewhere the fire had become cautious. In the controversy over the Hindu and Chinese liturgies, the Society backed off and settled for honest, Europeanized plodding in the missions and for diplomacy in Rome. Ignatius, convinced of his course, might have acted otherwise.

In China the attempt at adaptation was ended. In India it was crushed. In Paraguay it was dead.

Several ecclesiastics, trying to move with the times or at least be tolerated, were preaching a bland piety and a generously tolerant morality, a Christianity without spine. Vocations declined: the Benedictines dropped fifty percent. In 1789 over fifty Benedictine monasteries had no more than three monks apiece. In contrast, the Society's vocations increased 2,500 between 1710 and 1750. This was nowhere near the increase it had enjoyed in other forty-year periods. Nonetheless, the Philosophers singled out the Jesuits as the main obstacle to the eradication of the Catholic Church.

The Society surely had opposition from the Philosophers in France and from churchmen in Rome, but that was nothing new. What eventually made the opposition unbeatable was the gradual unification of the kings of Europe. They threatened to separate themselves from the Roman Church if the pope did not wipe out the Jesuits.

As Europe had grown from its Roman and barbaric infancy, the Church had been able to talk to kings as a father who had the last word, "Excommunication." But Henry VIII in England and some of the dukes of Germany had proved that one could live, even prosper, without the friendship of Peter. By the late eighteenth century the pope was a mere pawn on the royal bargaining tables of Europe and to some an irritating foreign intrusion.

But to a king jealous of his borders and his personal prowess, the infiltration of an international papal organization like the Society was intolerable.

It began in Portugal. In September 1758 an attempt had been made on the king's life, and the Marques de Pombal did not hesitate to use that attack in his plan to separate the Portuguese Church from Rome. By January all Jesuits in Portugal had been put under house arrest and all their property was confiscated in the name of the king. In April Joseph I ordered the eviction of the traitorous Society from his realm, except those willing to renounce their Jesuit vows. Fifteen hundred of the seventeen hundred Jesuits in Portugal and Paraguay chose exile. Of those who remained, about one hundred and fifty were in the royal dungeons.

Once the Jesuits were out of the way, Pombal gave the papal nuncio four days to get out of Portugal.

In France the movement was longer in focusing but no less effective. On August 6, 1761 Parliament ordered that the works of twenty-three Jesuits including Bellarmine and Lessius be publicly burned as destructive of morality and that the Society, in view of its evil effects on youth, could no longer receive novices. There is little new under the sun: from the Agora of Socrates to the Reichstag of Hitler the victims and the means of suppression have been the same. The Parliament further decreed that in towns where there were other schools the Jesuits should close their colleges by October 1, 1761. In places without other schools the Jesuit colleges could remain open until the following spring while new schools were being established.

In August 1762 the Society of Jesus was barred from France and her colonies and all its buildings were confiscated. Each Jesuit had to withdraw from his community and no Jesuit could teach anywhere in France unless he first took a vow repudiating the Society's rule and its vicious moral teachings. Three thousand Jesuits were dispersed. Some went to other orders, some to private homes, some to the missions, some--as was soon to be the only alternative to laicization--went to Poland. Paradoxically, it was a triumph both for the puritanical Jansenists on the right and for the Philosophers on the left.

In Spain the expulsion was both more dramatic and more efficient. On two separate nights, March 31 and April 2 of 1767, precisely at midnight, every Jesuit house in Spain was surrounded and the Jesuits were evicted with nothing more than their breviaries and the clothes on their backs. With these two quick strokes 188 colleges and thirty-one seminaries were emptied of twenty-seven hundred Spanish Jesuits. Within a year twenty-three hundred more were evicted from their missions and sent back to Europe.

When it was done, Choiseul, the architect of the French Suppression, received a letter from Manuel de Roda, his counterpart in Spain: "We have killed the son. Now nothing remains for us to do except to carry out a like action against the mother, our Holy Roman Church."

Thousands upon thousands of dispossessed Jesuits from houses all over Europe and from mission stations all over the world were shipped to Italy, dumped, and told to fend for themselves. The efforts of a Spanish Jesuit, Saint Joseph Pignatelli deserve far greater attention than they are given here. For twenty-four years he fed, lodged, and tried to resettle these men who had depended on the Society all their lives and had followed it in obedience even to its extinction.

It is hard to imagine the courts of Europe so blind to the intellectual suicide they were committing. Within ten years they had annihilated over six hundred colleges, one hundred and fifty seminaries, twenty universities. They had driven out twenty thousand professors, artists, mathematicians, parish priests, and playwrights. In a smaller way it was an act of blind hatred and self-destruction comparable to Hitler's up-rooting of the Jews.

On June 8, 1773 after delaying as long as he could but strangled by the threats of the kings of Europe, Pope Clement XIV--in the name of peace in the Church and to avoid the secession of all Europe--signed the brief Dominus ac Redemptor which dissolved the Society of Jesus throughout the world.

With one signature twenty-three thousand men were dispossessed of the life they had vowed to live forever.

The Society of Jesus was dead.

Well, not quite dead.

Because of Russia's share in the first partition of Poland, two hundred Jesuits and all the colleges of the Polish and Lithuanian provinces suddenly found themselves within the realm of Empress Catherine the Great. Without much enthusiasm for their Roman religion, the empress nonetheless valued the Jesuit contribution to the cultural life of her people. Most probably she also did not like to be told what to do by some little man down in Rome! She therefore declared that the Decree of Suppression not be promulgated in her empire.

With a perverse kind of benevolence she intended to keep the Society of Jesus alive. Furthermore, she swore that she would force all Catholics within White Russia to join the Orthodox Church unless the pope left "her" Jesuits alone.

Schism is to popes what midnight was to Cinderella. So Clement relented, perhaps even with a sigh of relief. Not only were the Jesuits allowed to continue, but they built a house of studies and began to receive former Jesuits and new candidates from all over the world. What's more, they elected a vicar-general, Stanislaw Czerniewicz, an old-time tightrope walker.

During the thirty years that the Society had been suppressed, France was rocked by her revolution and the accession of Napoleon Bonaparte. And along the eastern seaboard of the New World thirteen British colonies had become the United States of America.

John Carroll had been made the first bishop of the United States with his residence in Baltimore. As a former Jesuit he had three goals: to maintain a loose organization of ex-Jesuits in the States to be ready when the Society was restored, to build a college for Catholic laymen at Georgetown to be staffed with former Jesuits, and to maintain a definite connection between these former Jesuits and Rome.

The restless need for rebirth gradually began to spread. One cardinal wrote to a friend, "There was a time when, even though I backed the Jesuits, it seemed a little on the fanatical side to say that the Church could not live without them, since she had lived without them for so many centuries. . . . I believed then, and I believe now that the Church lives very badly without the Jesuits. If I were master, I would reestablish them tomorrow. "

Fortunately the new pope, Pius VII, was of the same mind and gave explicit approval to the Society in White Russia and approved requests from "holding" groups like the Fathers of the Sacred Heart to reaffiliate themselves with the Jesuits in eastern Poland. Thus while Napoleon was marching past him on his self-destructive way to Moscow, the Jesuit general was slowly putting together, piece by piece, the new Society of Jesus.

In 1814 when Napoleon had been defeated and ousted from power, the pope returned to Rome from his French captivity and on August 7, after saying Mass at the altar of St. Ignatius in the Church of the Gesu, he published the bull Sollicitudo Omnium reinstating the Society of Jesus throughout the world.

Peter de Smet, 1801-1873   *Friend of Sitting Bull*

I do not like the resurrection of the Jesuits. They have a general, now in Russia, in correspondence with the Jesuits in the United States who are more numerous than everybody knows. Shall we not have regular swarms of them here, in as many disguises as only a king of the gypsies can assume, dressed as printers, publishers, writers and schoolmasters? If ever there was a body of men who merited eternal damnation on earth and in hell, it is this Society of Loyola's. Nevertheless, we are compelled by our system of religious toleration to offer them asylum. But if they do not put the purity of our elections on a severe trial, it will be a wonder.

Thus former president John Adams wrote to President Thomas Jefferson on May 6, 1816.

Among this damnable crew, of course, were Jean de Brebeuf and Isaac Jogues who had arrived in the New World before the Adams family. It included Jacques Marquette who had discovered the Mississippi River which the president was eager to purchase. It included Eusebio Kino who for twenty-four years rode the length and breadth of Arizona on horseback building the first cattle industry to feed the Indians. Kino would one day have a statue in the Hall of Fame along with Adams and Jefferson. It included Anthony Kohlmann who was called to the deathbed of the presidents' old friend Tom Paine.

Also in this hellish company was Peter de Smet whom more than one American president would personally request for help. De Smet was the only man in America who could bring the justly rebellious western Indians to peace.

De Smet was a great hulk of a man. His brother Jesuits called him "Samson." During his studies at White Marsh, Maryland and then at Florissant, Missouri he had always been restless. It was this restlessness that made him run away from home in Belgium to be a missionary to the Indians.

Even in the seminary he could not keep still, and so in his spare time he began a school for Indian boys near St. Louis. He rode out beating a drum, and the boys followed him into the school. Getting them there and keeping them there were two different things. Books and hoeing and prayers were not what they'd expected, so they ran away. They were hauled back several times. But then the nearby tribes, fed up with the continuing encroachments of the whites, moved further west from St. Louis.

De Smet looked around him; ten years wasted. To make his life even more wretched, he was afflicted with some skin disease that kept spreading and refused to heal. Finally in despair, he asked to leave the Society. For awhile he served as chaplain to a convent, but that was too small a job for his big heart and big body. He could not resist the call from his childhood, and he came back to Missouri.

Then the right call came. Some Indians in Nebraska asked for a Jesuit priest, and off he went. He feasted with them on dog and starved with them on acorns and moss. He watched the women drudge and the men gamble and the children starve. He saw men literally barter away their own children for whiskey.

De Smet was a doctor, teacher, priest, and diplomat for his Indians. He rode fearlessly into camps of Sioux and demanded peace, but he was helpless against the whiskey. He stormed around like Carrie Nation, battering in the barrels, but it would have been easier to baptize Beelzebub than to shackle Demon Rum. He who had dreams of new Reductions in the Northwest finally had to admit that he had been beaten, again.

Then a group of Flathead Indians came from Montana and asked for a priest. Peter de Smet was definitely available. When he arrived in the mountains between the Rockies and the Pacific, he began by making a circuit of the land and then rode back to St. Louis to raise money and men. So persuasive was he on both counts that in 1841 he returned with supplies and six more Jesuits and began to do what he did best: building. He built a sawmill, workshops, a flour mill. Farms began to spread and the tepees of the former nomads began to cluster around his centers.

Just like the letters of Brebeuf and Jogues and Marquette, De Smet's letters were sent back to Europe and circulated in parishes and schools all over the continent. After he had made another circuit from Idaho to Vancouver, he decided that it was time to return to Europe for more strong backing and more strong backs. Because of the letters, his fame preceded him, and like Paul Bunyan he went from church to church telling his stories. And when he finished this different kind of circuit, he returned to the Pacific Northwest with a boatload full of men and goods. The map of his journeys looks like the web of some jubilant spider. By canoe and steamboat, on horse and on foot, by dogsled and snowshoes he sprinkled churches and clusters of homes like the sower of good seed.

Then suddenly the shock: orders to return to St. Louis and to hulk his big body behind a desk. So successful had he been at supporting his missions that he had been made the province treasurer and fund raiser for all the Jesuit missions from the

Great Lakes to Louisiana.

It was a bitter blow. He was not yet fifty. He could keep up with the best and youngest on the trail. No one got along with the Indians as he did. He was energetic, hardworking, zealous, experienced, popular. But he had always lacked control and moderation. He had opened the mission; now steadier hands had to mold and coordinate its growth.

So whenever the mission was starved for men and money, De Smet went back to Germany, France, Holland, Belgium. Sixteen more times he crossed the Atlantic and brought back a hundred more priests to the United States. And whenever he got back to his desk in St. Louis, there were letters from Santa Fe asking him to work there; from the governor of the Washington Territory asking him to help survey for a new railroad; from President Lincoln asking help to keep the Sioux and Osage from raiding government posts. Reporters were always harassing him for stories about how he directed Brigham Young to the Great Salt Lake, about his friends Kit Carson and Jim Bridger, about his proposal to make Yellowstone into a national park.

But his greatest concern was the Indians. As the white settlers gradually drove the Indians out of their own land to get the gold or timber or farming space, the mood of the tribes smoldered and flared. Suddenly starvation and betrayal and frustration exploded in raids on the white settlements and massacres of their inhabitants. After months of savagery on both sides, a peace powwow was finally arranged and ten thousand Indians converged on Fort Laramie, Wyoming. The government go-between was Peter de Smet. He begged the Indians to go back to their reservations pledging that the white man would surely keep his word this time.

In 1849 the gold miners whooped into the Rockies and drove the Indians from their lands. Blood flowed again, tepees were burned, and the Indians straggled off to another wilderness.

In 1861 when he was sixty years old, De Smet made a winter trip into the mountains to see what he could do to help. What he found was appalling. The villages he had spent half his life creating had become ghost towns. Heartsick, he returned to his ledgers in St. Louis.

Still again, when he was sixty-eight he crossed the Badlands to confer with Sitting Bull and promise, hopefully, that the white men would indeed stay off the reservation lands.

He was growing tired. He was weighed down by age and the toll of a lifetime of travel. He was weighed down by hundreds of promises he had made in good faith and had seen the white men break again and again.

In the end gold was discovered on the Sioux reservation in Dakota, gold he himself had discovered years before and covered up, knowing what it would do to the rapacious whites and the Indians' need to be left alone. The news now spread like a plague and Sitting Bull, unable to keep feeding his children on broken promises, took up the war hatchet and slaughtered General Custer and all of his men at the Little Big Horn. But Peter de Smet was not called to bribe Sitting Bull with false promises this time. Peter de Smet was dead.

Throughout his life, despite a history of dreams achieved and shattered, Peter de Smet had been a big man.

Gerard Manley Hopkins, 1844-1899   *Jesuit Poet*

Gerard Manley Hopkins was a man none of his lay friends could believe would ever enter as fascist an organization as they imagined the Society of Jesus to be. He was a man of enormous poetic gifts and his sensitivity was surely doomed to perish in an order whose austerities and militarism reduced all its men to calculators and systematizers. His friend Canon Dixon wrote frequent letters begging him to return to his senses and leave the Society. Even today many critics read into his later poems, the so-called "terrible sonnets," Hopkins' doubts about his vocation and his faith. His diaries give ample proof that they are mistaken.

Hopkins had been brought up in strict Victorian rectitude, and yet he was spunky enough to stand up to schoolmasters when they whipped him unjustly. The combination is worth remembering. When he was converted from Anglicanism and baptized by Cardinal Newman at age twenty-two, he had the typical young convert's passion to be a touch holier than the holy. With Newman's advice and approval, he entered the Jesuit novitiate.

To anyone who has known good but somewhat excessive converts, it is not too surprising that when Hopkins entered the novitiate, he burned his youthful poems in a burst of ascetic fervor. He left the world entirely behind him. Even later in his life he worried too scrupulously about taking time from teaching and grading papers to write poems. He was fearful, too, of the notoriety that might come to him if the poems were published. To an outsider, especially to a nonbeliever, such reticence is damnable.

In 1878 Hopkins wrote to Dixon, "What I have written I burnt before I became a Jesuit and resolved to write no more, as not belonging to my profession, unless it were the wish of my superiors; so for seven years I wrote nothing but two or three presentation pieces which occasion called for. But when in the winter of '75 the Deutschland was wrecked in the mouth of the Thames and five Franciscan nuns were drowned, I was affected by the account and happening to say so to my rector, he said that he wished someone would write a poem on the subject. On this hint, I set to work and, though my hand was out at first, produced one." The poem he produced was perhaps to be his most famous, "The Wreck of the Deutschland."

To be fair to the critics we must admit that this classic poem was submitted to a Jesuit periodical, The Month, kept for awhile, and then rejected. It was neither the first nor the last time a Jesuit editor was blind to genius. We gave Galileo a rather bad time, and Ricci and De Nobili and James Joyce and Teilhard de Chardin. But if, as a Jesuit, I claim brotherhood with Jesuit saints, I must also claim brotherhood with Jesuit bunglers.

It should be clear that a Jesuit does not take his vows to critics or even to a particular inept superior but to Jesus Christ who himself went innocently but obediently to an undeserved cross. These vows to Christ are pledged in a Society which requires a man to actually live that prayer of St. Ignatius which every novice knows by heart before he's been in the Society a week:

Take and receive, O Lord, my liberty.
Take all my will, my mind, my memory.
Do Thou direct and govern all and sway.
Do what Thou wilt; command, and I obey.
Only Thy grace and love on me bestow.
Possessing these, all riches I forego.

As with all love, to him who understands, no explanation is necessary; to him who does not understand, no explanation is possible.

The prayer of St. Ignatius is hardly an anthem for the marketplace or for the editorial rooms of slick magazines. But Hopkins had not become a Jesuit to be a businessman or even a poet. His vows should have given evidence even to his disbelieving friends that for him at least there was Someone more important in his life than poetry.

But when an outsider like Hopkins' friend Robert Bridges sees such foolishness, he cannot begin to understand its motivation since he denies the Reality on whom the motives rest. Hopkins tried to explain it to Dixon who was a clergyman and should have understood. "As for myself, I have not only made my vows publicly two and twenty times, but I make them to myself every day, so that I should be black with perjury if I drew back now. And beyond that, I can say with Peter: 'To whom shall I go? You have the words of eternal life.'" In another letter he says that he leaves the questions like the publication of his poems to his superiors and tries to live by trusting in the providence of God. "If you value what I write, as I do myself, much more does the Lord. "

In 1879 Hopkins tried to explain to his friend Bridges that "Feeling, love in particular, is the great moving power of verse, and the only Person that I am in love with, seldom, especially now, stirs my heart sensibly. And when he does, I cannot always 'make capital' of it; it would be sacrilege to do so. "

Hopkins was ordained in 1877 and served in Jesuit parishes in London, Oxford, Liverpool, and Glasgow. He then taught classics in the Jesuit secondary school at Stonyhurst until he was appointed professor of Greek at University College, Dublin in 1884.

In the early years his poems celebrated the "inscape" of things, their self-ness, their unique individuality, that "freshness deep-down things" which may, indeed, be God. He reveled in their obstinate differences: "Glory be to God for dappled things . . . all things counter, original, spare, strange. " His poems were a tension between a childlike delight in the sensuous world and the simple austerity in his religious spirit. To embody this tension in words he welded the rhythms of Welsh poems, Old English, and nursery rhymes into a cadence he called "sprung rhythm. " And beneath all the bleary film of industrial life he saw Christ "lovely in limbs, and lovely in eyes not his" playing "to the Father through the features of men's faces. "

But his later years show that he, too, suffered a martyrdom, not of blood as many of his brothers had, nor even of his talents as many of his friends believed he did, but of the spirit. Like Ignatius at Manresa, he moved into the dark night of the soul.

He became sick in Dublin. His work became a treadmill. The senseless hatreds between his Irish and British brother Jesuits wounded his childlike soul which expected far better of them. Even those who did not snigger at his scrupulosity seemed to consider him little more than a harmless eccentric. In the "terrible sonnets" he saw himself as doing nothing for

Christ, "breeding not one work that wakes," and he felt that
he was stretched "on a rack where, self-wrung, self-strung,
sheathed and shelterless, thoughts against thoughts in groans
grind. "

His diaries are as grim: "Life here is as dank as ditch water: at least I know that I am reduced to great weakness by
diarrhea, which lasts too, as if I were poisoned. . . . I take
up a languid pen, being down with diarrhea and vomiting
brought on by yesterday's heat and the long hours in the confessional. . . . But I never could write. Time and spirit are
wanting. One is so fagged, so harried and gallied up and down.
And the drunkards go on drinking, and the filthy as scripture
says, are filthy still; human nature is inveterate. Would that
I had seen the last of it. "

And yet at the very time he was most despondent, when
the drudgery of marking exam papers was threatening his eye-
sight, and his scrupulosity over the grades he gave was sense-
lessly tormenting him, he wrote in a notebook quoting the
Spiritual Exercises, "'And all the other things on earth (are
to be used insofar as they bring man to fulfill the purpose of
his creation: to praise and serve God.)' Take it that weakness, ill-health, every cross is a help. 'The chalice which
my Father gives me, shall I not drink it?' God, make us in-
different--with the elective will. Not the effective will, especially; but the affective will will follow. . . . I must ask God to
strengthen my faith. "

To him who does not understand, no explanation is possible.

In a sonnet he wrote on St. Alphonsus Rodriguez, an ob-
scure Jesuit brother who was canonized, he contrasted the
glorious and the hidden martyrdoms: "But be the war within,
the brand we wield unseen, the heroic breast not outward-
steeled, earth hears no hurtle then from fiercest fray. . . .
God (that hew mountain and continent, earth, all, out; who,
with trickling increment, veins violet and tall trees makes
more and more) could crown career with conquest. . . . "

His was not a martyrdom without a crown, but as with
most holy men, it was a crown he never saw. It is surely

remarkable that poetry so hidden from the world should now
be praised throughout the world.

All martyrdoms are not dramatic. Many are not understood.

Miguel Pro, 1891-1927   *Jesuit Clown*

One of the criteria for selecting the Jesuits who appear on these
pages was, quite simply, that I liked them. And Miguel Pro is
the one I like best of all, partly because he was an actor, but
mostly because he loved life so much and lived it so zestfully
that the cruel brevity of it seems less unfair.

From his earliest years he was a mimic, an actor, a clown.
He played the guitar and set people roaring with funny songs.
He left school before finishing his studies. He went to daily
Mass because his whole family did. When his two sisters decided to become nuns, he ran away from home for almost a
week. But then things changed. An atheist dictator became president of Mexico, shot 160 priests and hundreds of laymen within a few months, and forbade any Mexican to attend Mass under
pain of death.

So Miguel Pro decided to become a Jesuit.

Because of the persecution, Miguel was educated in seminaries in California, Spain, and Nicaragua and was finally ordained in Belgium in 1925. Through the whole course of studies
he had been such a cutup, such a buffoon, that many men in
his own year never realized that he suffered constantly from
insomnia and agonizing abdominal pains for which no remedy
could be found. As the years of pain dragged on, Miguel knew
that even if he were willing to remain quiet and alternate his
time between some undemanding job and longer and longer stays
in the hospital, he probably had very few years left to live.

So Miguel Pro decided to live his remaining years as a priest
in the atheistic police state of Mexico.

At first, because he had been so long out of the country,
he was unknown to any of the ten thousand secret police and he

worked practically undisturbed. He brazenly walked the streets from one secret Mass to another, gave three hundred communions a day, twelve hundred on feast days. He formed a group of 150 young Catholic leaders, formed whole regiments of catechists to replace the Catholic schools which had been closed, gave retreats--now to fifty taxi drivers, now to eighty civil servants. For two years it was an endless round of baptisms, confessions, weddings. He begged food for families whose fathers and sons were in prison or executed, and within a year of his return he had more than a hundred families completely dependent on him.

One can't be responsible for such a joyous upheaval and still remain anonymous. But when the police finally discovered who he was, they had a far more difficult job finding out where he was, and he resolved to give them the chase of their lives. He had a case filled with disguises, false mustaches, putty noses, spectacles of all kinds, costumes from dungarees to morning coats, and a rubber face that could flicker from peon to patrician in an instant, no matter what the clothes.

His insolence was limitless. He grimly marched the streets with a huge police dog, and the police were so numerous they couldn't tell whether he was one of them or not. On several occasions when he was jailed, he sat drooling and gibbering in his cell until he was released as a harmless half-wit. Once he persuaded his jailer to let him escape, only to turn up the next morning loaded with blankets, food, and cigarettes for the other prisoners, half of whose confessions he had heard the previous evening. In fact he wandered in and out of prisons so brazenly that most of the jailers presumed he must be a secret policeman or an official interrogator.

One day he was approaching a house to say Mass and noticed too late that plainclothes detectives were guarding the door. He stopped, took out a notebook, noted the address, and swaggered up to the door muttering grimly, "Something fishy going on here!" He put his hand under his lapel, flipped it so fast that they couldn't see that he had no badge, and pushed his way into the house. The detectives saluted him and stepped out of his way. When he had warned his friends, he strutted out the door and down the street like a matador ignoring a bull.

Another time he was leaving a house after Mass and met a detective at the door. "There's a priest in that house," the officer whispered. Miguel looked appalled. "Good heavens, no!" and like a good citizen followed the detective back in to help search the apartment, opening closets, poking under beds, making helpful suggestions, and casually picking up the Mass kit he had left behind. After awhile, Pro looked fussily at his watch, apologized for being unable to stay longer, and went off with the case in his hand promising that he would stop by later to see if the priest had been found.

Once when two policemen came to his father's house to arrest him, he asked them if he couldn't stop for just one last drink at a cafe. While they sat there, he got them so drunk that he convinced them they had a false lead. Whenever police chased him down the streets, he darted round a corner, threw off his jacket, rumpled his hair, lit a cigarette and, when the police rounded the corner, pointed off in the direction the priest had taken. Or if he saw a pretty girl, he excused himself, grabbed her and began necking until the detectives had gone off. On another occasion he flatly refused to come to jail because if he did, he would be unable to hear the confession of the detective's dying mother. He sent him off to tell the mother he'd be there the following morning with communion.

Underground presses had printed thousands of stickers bearing slogans and Catholic propaganda which were slapped up everywhere. While Pro was carrying a load of these stickers from the printer, he would tuck one up under the back of his collar and leave it dangling there as he walked along the streets and boarded a streetcar. Grinning like the kind of idiot children would play a practical joke on, he'd parade around like a walking sermon.

It is hard to believe that he lasted two years.

The end came suddenly. One afternoon General Obregon, a candidate for the presidency, was ambushed, and although he was unhurt, the secret police used the attack as an occasion for a reign of terror. In the middle of the night a small army surrounded Father Pro's house. They dragged Miguel to prison and kept him under constant guard trying to force him to confess a murder attempt on Obregon. Whenever they took him back to his cell, he quietly began where he left off hearing the confessions of his fellow prisoners.

On the third day an officer unlocked the door of his cell and called him. Presuming that he was being called for trial, he got up and followed. But instead of going toward the court house, the officers marched him out to the prison yard. Ashamedly, the officer asked his forgiveness. Realizing that he had already been "tried," Miguel said to him, "I do more than forgive you. I thank you."

When asked if he had a last request, he said he would like a few moments to kneel down and pray. Then he stood to the firing squad.

In a loud voice he said, "May God have mercy on you and bless you. God, you know I am innocent. I forgive my enemies with all my heart."

Looking small and insignificant this insidious Jesuit raised his crucifix in one hand and his rosary in the other. As the five rifles fired, he shouted in an unquavering voice, "Viva Cristo Rey!"

He fell in a heap, and an officer came forward and fired a shot into his head.

Jesuits of the Present   II

Daniel Lord, 1888-1954   *The Jesuit Who Never Grew Old*

Dan Lord's college years were like a late show musical, rac-
coon coats, pennants, and "The Varsity Drag. " Everything in
the world was against his becoming a Jesuit. Everything but
One.

By the time he was a college senior, he had published articles in national magazines and had a brilliant college dramatic
career behind him. He had fallen out of love with a girl he had
been going with for two years, but he had an offer from "a
synthetically blonde divorcee" to join her in a cross-country
vaudeville team. Besides, he had lost his faith.

But he had also met a Jesuit scholastic named Claude Pernin
who moderated the college magazine and ruthlessly forced
Lord to polish and hone his style, his stories, and his mind.
So while his mother very quietly and effectively handled the
problem of the divorcee, Mr. Pernin very quietly and effectively handled the problem of the faith.

Dan was fairly settled on a law career; his world was good
and his life was at peace. But then one day Pernin asked him
where he was going to law school. "God knows why I gave the

completely unintended and utterly absurd answer: 'Oh, I don't know. But sometimes I have thought I might be a Jesuit.' Even as I said it the whole thing sounded ridiculous. I did not think I'd be a Jesuit. I did not want to be a Jesuit; in fact, I could think of nothing I wanted less. The life had little appeal for me. Jesuits who had taught me had not much impressed my young arrogance. I was having much too good a time in life. Though for a moment I was interested in no particular girl, there were a number of charming young ladies on my horizon. 'If,' I said with a real chill in my voice, 'you want to do me a favor, you'll regard the whole thing as nonsense and drop the subject for good.'"

On July 26, 1909 Dan Lord entered the novitiate at Florissant, Missouri.

For a few years his training was typical; that is, at least typical enough that I who entered forty-two years after him nod knowingly when I read his autobiography, Played by Ear. And a novice today would recognize the core of the story if not the sylvan frills and thrills. But at the end of his juniorate Lord's experience became nontypical for awhile. He contracted typhoid fever and was too weak after his recovery to begin philosophy right away. So he went for a year to work with Father Gareshé at The Queen's Work, a magazine for the members of the national Sodality of Our Lady. It was not a wasted year; The Queen's Work was to occupy a great many more years of Lord's life.

When he finally began philosophy at St. Louis University, Dan Lord and his friend Frank Quinn put on the first of many, many musicals they would produce together as Jesuits.

During the three years he spent as a regent or teaching scholastic in St. Louis, he taught both in the university and in the high school (at the same time), prefected corridors, moderated the newly formed ROTC, ran the band, and put on plays and musicals. Your typical regency--1918 or 1958 or 1988.

While he was studying theology, the sisters at a nearby grammar school asked if he would put on a play with their pupils. Their impossible little stage sent him pleading to Lou Egan, a quiet, one-word-at-a-time scholastic who seemed to know something about electricity. Dan made his pitch, gave Lou the entire budget of twenty dollars, and didn't see him again till the dress rehearsal. When he got backstage, he was flabbergasted by the collection of kitchen chairs, cracker tins, tobacco cans, bed sheets, buckets, and other assembled pieces of junk. But the lighting was beautiful. Again, this was the first of many shows Dan would do with a man he praised in a little book called The Jesuit with the Magic Hands.

After ordination, Dan Lord took charge of The Queen's Work, an enterprise which consisted of a typewriter, two Jesuits, and a secretary who was about to quit. He was also responsible for the Sodality, a national organization which was to all intents and purposes dead. His first article was "Shall We Let the Sodality Die?" and he followed that with a steady stream of articles, not pious little stories, but taunts, challenges, and accusations that he knew young people could only answer with anger, then thought, then action. He conned the best Jesuits he knew into writing articles; interviewed every "big" Catholic he could corner. He pulled controversies out from under the rug where even adult Catholics were just as happy to leave them: race prejudice, slum children, persecution in Mexico, obscenity in films. This was not in the 70's but in the 30's. He dared young people to think, and he dared them to come alive and do something about what they thought.

A priest friend once asked him, "Aren't you afraid sometimes, Dan, that you're asking a little too much of young people? Here you're asking them to be interested in everything under the sun and to lead not just good lives but saintly lives. Isn't it too much, and can't it be discouraging to them?"

"Leo," he said, "you can't ask too much of youth--it's impossible."

"Well, you've certainly never talked down to them. You treat them as if they're adults."

And Dan Lord replied, "They very nearly are."

Before Dan Lord was finished, The Queen's Work was being sent to one hundred thousand readers.

Then it was the moribund Sodality's turn. The purpose of the Sodality, like the Society, was to sanctify each member through his work for others. Lord's goal was to make young people "vocal Christians." But service is merely humanistic, not Christian, unless the worker has a personal relationship with God. How to take this formalistic, sparsely populated organization and use it to draw fire from heaven and cast fire on the earth? There were a few healthy pockets here and there, good men and women trying, but they felt very much alone. So Dan Lord decided to pull together the small live cells into local conventions and leadership workshops. He eventually built these into the national Summer Schools of Catholic Action which drew sodalists and moderators from all over the country. Within eighteen years one hundred thousand people had attended the SSCA.

A newspaper article described Lord's work, "The new Catholic youth movement with its all-embracing Catholic activities, its inculcation of personal and social sanctity, its direction of the enthusiasm of American youth into Catholic ways, has been the most significant Catholic enterprise in the U. S. in our times." "

Nothing attracts critics like success. Like Ricci and de Nobili and every other Jesuit worth his corn bread, Dan Lord was criticized. He was a vulgarian, a clerical showman, superficial, crude. And the Sodality was too big. How could so many kids develop a real spiritual life? How many were really involved in the social apostolates? To which Dan sometimes responded, "You know the old recipe for rabbit stew? First, you gotta catch your rabbit. "

On the side he wrote pamphlets. During his lifetime, they sold fifteen million copies. One Chicago bookstore sold twenty thousand copies of one pamphlet the day it came out. And letters; one time when he was in the hospital, he answered sixty letters in a day. He also wrote two syndicated columns every week, besides writing for The Queen's Work--and editing it. Dan Lord was spendthrift with words; over the years he averaged about twenty thousand words a month for publication.

And the talks. He never knew when to stop. He'd speak awhile, accusing his young audience of things they were only half guilty of, challenging them to the joy of thinking. And then he would throw the whole thing open to their observations, questions, and difficulties. Then he'd head back to his office, haul out his battered portable, and hammer out another article or pamphlet for kids. He was the first to admit that the articles were "really written by the kids themselves. . . . They were my teachers."

While all these plates were spinning in the air, Dan Lord was also writing the script, music, and lyrics for at least one original musical every year. He directed and choreographed them as well. Each one of the musicals had some kind of apostolic thrust lurking not far beneath the kliegs and taps and spangles. In March of 1936 it was a pageant for the hundredth anniversary of the island of Jamaica. The next year, the three hundredth anniversary of Milwaukee. Then "A Salute to Canada" at the shrine of Jean de Brebeuf in Midland, Ontario. This pageant had a cast of five hundred actors and dancers including the full Canadian Ballet and Canadian Symphony Orchestra!

When he wrote and directed the pageant for the 250th anniversary of Detroit, a Jewish physician wrote to a newspaper, "Much time have I wasted deprecating and ridiculing those who speak of big men and great men. . . . It took an outsider, an outlander, a Father Lord, boldly to simmer out the decency that dwells in all men. . . . I have wondered what in the world was meant by the words 'brotherhood of man.' Father Lord showed it as I have never seen it before. I wish Father Lord would live in Detroit. One felt, with the seventeen thousand people who viewed the performance that night, a sense of the holiness of Father Lord. There is a singing in my heart that was not there before. That night I saw a miracle."

In the 30's a Hollywood producer made him a standing offer of fifty thousand dollars a year, but he answered that there wasn't enough money in the world to lure him away from what he was doing.

In the early 1950's the pace began to catch up with Father Lord. In January, 1954 when he went for a checkup, the doctor told him that he had cancer, that, in fact, he probably had had it for eight or nine years. Dan's only question was, "Can I keep up with my work?"

And he did. Talks in Denver, Milwaukee, Detroit, Toronto. Two books, The Man Who Was Really Santa Claus and his autobiography, Played by Ear. At times, when the pain was too bad, he'd stop for a day or two. Then he was off to Toronto for his pageant, "Joy for the World." He worked on it from his bed at St. Michael's Hospital during the day and then rehearsed it each night at a downtown theater. When the rehearsals with twelve hundred actors moved into the Toronto coliseum, he put it together from a wheelchair, his secretary on one side taking notes and a nurse on the other giving him sedatives.

Then he had to go into the hospital for the final time. When he lapsed into delirium, he was still giving orders: "Get going on this right away . . . speed it up . . . hurry!" Even at the edge of death there was not enough time to finish all the things he wanted to do.

The best summary came from his friend and colleague, Leo Wobido, S. J.: "His happy gift of zeal was, like that of Francis Xavier, a fatal gift. Like his great hero, Xavier, he too during his stretches of delirium on his deathbed was doing big things and planning even bigger ones."

I had thought to call this section, "The Priest Who Never Sat Still." Then I thought it should be "The Priest Who Always Went Big." And then I thought I'd leave it as it was.

He had a natural gift of tongues. His parents taught him their native German and he learned English growing up in Weehawken, New Jersey. He spoke Latin in the novitiate and all the textbooks in philosophy and theology were in Latin. During philosophy studies in Canada he picked up French scarcely realizing he was doing it. When he organized the glee club of the Culion Leper Colony in the Philippines, he taught the basses in Visayan and the tenors in Tagalog. He taught the very old in Spanish and the very young in English. In the Japanese prison camps of Mindanao he learned Japanese.

He was a quiet, energetic man. Deep-chested and muscular as a baseball catcher, he thought nothing of swimming the Hudson River with his three brothers from Jersey to the New York side. When he entered the Society of Jesus, Carl Hausmann was a lone wolf, working on the grounds, building benches, practicing his violin in the woodshed. He was not a grumpy man, just calm, with humor in his eyes and a patient grin. In theology studies at Woodstock, Maryland they say he kept silence in seven languages.

After tertianship he was granted the wish of his life, to go to the Philippines. It was not quite what he'd dreamed. While he was procurator and teacher of Greek in the novitiate there, he studied native dialects at night under a kerosene lamp. He studied stripped to the waist with a towel around his neck to absorb the sweat. He balanced the books, barely, and listened to the lizards and bugs and roaches. Walking out to teach catechism, he felt his cassock glued to his back before he hit the road in front of the seminary. He chopped cogon grass with the laborers and blushed when he could pay them only fifty cents a day. He woke up to the morning rain for six months on end. And he never complained. The reason was simple; he loved it. And the Filipinos loved him. So with the Ignatian itch for the greater service, he volunteered for the Culion Leper Colony.

He had read somewhere that lepers were the happiest people in the world because, with nothing left, they turned completely to God. When he arrived at the island, he found that wasn't true. Lepers are like anybody else.

There were lepers whose physical revulsion at themselves had infected their spirits. They became shrewd, greedy, shrill, pouty, cruel. Many of them worked furiously in the sun, not out of a need for dignity or even out of ambition, but only so they could catch fever and die.

But there was sweetness too, especially in the children whose innocence had not yet been soured by the realization that they were doomed. The people's eyes at times were grateful; this priest spoke to each in his own language, sat with them dying, touched their hands. He was their one last hope of goodness in the world. He loved them.

So it was heart-wrenching when he was transferred to Mindanao; but he had made a vow, and he went. He went from living with lepers to living with headhunting Moros and negrito dwarfs who carried nasty little poisoned blowpipes. Some people putt-putted over the mountains in jitneys that civilization had long since thrown away; some rode through the passes on horseback; Belgians rode their bicycles. But because it was faster to go through the forest paths than by the roundabout roads, Carl walked.

It was in Mindanao that the war caught up with him. First the planes went over; then the mail stopped; then came the dull thud of artillery up the coast. Without air support the Philippine army began a slow, bloody retreat into the interior and established a base hospital at Impulatao. They carried the wounded there from all over the island. One day Carl Hausmann showed up and asked if he could help the dying since there was no chaplain at the hospital. Then and there he enlisted as an army chaplain. Two days later the army surrendered. Hausmann became a prisoner of war.

Army personnel were imprisoned inside a barbed wire pen in the Impulatao barrio. It wasn't bad at first, if you didn't need much food. But then they were transferred to the penal colony at Davao to work in the rice fields. This was very bad indeed, hunger, thirst, long days bent over in the broiling sun, and worst of all, dysentery. Hundreds of men slept together, sweating, shivering, turning yellow with hepatitis. For two years. Toward the end Carl measured out Mass wine with an eyedropper. Then the bread ran out. Then Mass stopped altogether.

With his body full of festering scabs from rice rash, Carl worked for others in the fields during his time off--because they were sick. A fellow chaplain later said, "Carl died partly because he gave his food away. We were getting two spoonfuls of rice every third day, and he gave his away. And the shame of it was that the men he gave it to weren't worthy of it. He gave it to the whiners, the weaklings. When they complained, he'd lean over and dump his ration in their cup, without a word. "

In late June, 1944 the Davao prisoners were shipped north to Luzon to work on a Japanese airfield with the survivors of Bataan and Corregidor. At night they could only pray and dream of food. But here Carl would say Mass, and it actually made his face radiant. With his gaunt body and sunken cheeks, the Catholics called him St. Joseph. Non-Catholics facetiously but more accurately called him the Holy Ghost. This impression of inner holiness emerging from the quiet man was shared by everyone in the camp. One survivor who knew him only slightly says, "Maybe he was too much at home with God. He was so thoroughly in the state of grace that it made the rest of us feel unclean, uncomfortable. It's not natural for a man to give away his food when he is starving, to work for someone else when he himself can hardly stand up. Holiness is an easy thing to hate, and he was holy, but . . . we liked him. "

Through three years of internment no one ever heard him complain or fight back or lose his temper, even when a prisoner stole his Mass kit and offered to sell it back, piece by piece.

Only once did he resist the guards.

One morning in November, 1944 in the courtyard of Bilibid Penitentiary in Manila, Carl was saying Mass for the prisoners when an air raid sounded. The men scurried for shelter, but Carl went on with Mass. A guard shoved him, but he went on staring at the host. The guard hit him with his rifle, but he would not move. In a rage, the guard began to club the priest again and again. The other prisoners ran shouting into the yard and as the guard turned to drive them back, Carl finished the consecration, consumed the sacred species, and went back to his cell.

Toward the middle of December, 1944 the Japanese shipped sixteen hundred prisoners off to Japan aboard the Oroyku Maru. American planes bombed and strafed the ship for a night and a day and drove it aground on the shore of Subic Bay. The planes hit the ship squarely with three bombs, and the prisoners made a mad rush for the ladders. The Japanese drove them back by firing point blank into their faces.

Then the Oroyku Maru caught fire. The Japanese jumped ship and the prisoners leaped overboard and swam ashore to escape. A division of Japanese infantry was waiting for them on the beach.

It sounds like a movie, but it happened.

For a week the prisoners were jammed into a tennis court without shelter, without food. Seven days later those still alive were packed into another freighter bound for Japan, but bombers found them again off Formosa and scored a direct hit on the forward hold. The Japanese looked down into the bloody welter of bodies and sealed the hold for forty-eight hours. The living were pinned under the dead in the darkness and morning brought the heat and the stench. When the ship finally limped into harbor, only seven of the five hundred men trapped in the hold were still alive. Hausmann lay on the deck and watched as the dead were hauled out in a wire loading net and dumped into a barge.

The rest of the voyage was so ghastly that one has to read three or four accounts of it before he can believe it actually happened. A half-cup of rice every three days. . . . The crew

going around every morning to haul out the dead. . . . Grudges
surfacing and men found dead with their stomachs slit open.
. . . A navy chaplain reading aloud from his bible, over and
over and over, while the men tried to shut the sound out of
their ears till the chaplain finally ran screaming for the ladder and had to be pulled down and tied up. . . . Flies and
stench and festering wounds and overflowing latrine cans. . . .
A man slashing his neighbor to death to drink his blood. . . .
Hunger and thirst, madness and despair.

It was in this corner of hell that Carl Hausmann made his
last confession, blessed himself, and died.

The last rule of St. Ignatius reads as follows: "As in the
whole of life, so also in death, everyone of the Society must
make it his effort to care that God our Lord be glorified and
served in him, and that those around be edified at least by
the example of his patience and fortitude. "

When Hausmann was dead, they stripped his body and gave
what clothes he had to the living. Then the boatswain tied a
rope around his knees and neck and called, "All right. Take
it away. " The rope tightened and the body of Carl Hausmann
rose slowly, gaunt and naked up through the hatch. The survivors heard his body dragged across the deck and stacked
near the rail to be dumped or used for fuel, they never found
out.

As the silence settled on them one sailor said, "It's tough.
He was a good man. He knew Japanese. "

Joseph O'Callahan, 1905-1964   *Congressional Medal of Honor*

World War II was almost over. Germany had surrendered.
The Japanese had fallen back atoll by atoll in the Pacific and
were about to lose the battle of Manila. Joe O'Callahan had
"fought" his war for two and a half years as a combat chaplain
on the U. S. S. Ranger, and he now had an easy job at Pearl
Harbor. He merely had to wait a few months to return to his

87

teaching at Holy Cross College. So he "listened to gripes, shuttled between men and their officers, arranged movies, and did all the picayune tasks given to that mother-psychologist-efficiency expert, the unmilitary moral officer."

But on March 2, 1945 with victory in the Pacific almost inevitable, Joe O'Callahan received orders to report as chaplain to another carrier, the U.S.S. Franklin. The following day they steamed out of Pearl Harbor to join a task force of sixteen carriers, eight battleships, sixteen cruisers, and sixty-three destroyers. The purpose of this flotilla was to knock out air bases on the mainland of Japan to cut casualties in the invasion of Okinawa and the mainland itself. The Japanese needed no radar to find a fleet of that size. And for at least a week Father O'Callahan spent most of his time hearing confessions.

On Saturday, March 17 the chaplain said Mass on the fo'c'sle for twelve hundred men. It wasn't Sunday or a holy day or even the fact that it was St. Patrick's day. It was the last Mass before combat.

Before sunrise on March 18 the planes of the Franklin took off to bomb the airfields of Kagoshima--paradoxically, the same place Francis Xavier had first landed in Japan. The carrier then zigzagged for ninety minutes before returning to the rendezvous point. It was the chaplain's job to man the loudspeakers throughout the day and give news reports of the progess of the missions in order to unify the spirit of the three-thousand-man operation. All day and into the night flights took off and returned till finally, at about 2:00 a.m. Father O'Callahan fell exhausted into his bunk. At three-thirty there was quiet. Around 6 a.m. the chaplain decided to grab some breakfast while he could.

Then it came.

Suddenly there was an explosion. Then another. "Quicker than the echo of the blast, the mind knows that the moment has come. Was it a Jap, a Kamikaze? Or one of our own bombs? A Tiny Tim rocket?" It had been one Japanese plane with two lucky hits. As he threw himself onto the deck, O'Callahan gave general absolution to the whole crew and his thoughts raced to the realization that whatever the cause the ship itself had become a huge floating bomb. There were a hundred planes on the flight and hangar decks, their tanks filled with hundreds of gallons of high octane gas. There were thousands of bombs, 1,000 and 2,000 pounds each, attached to the planes and stacked throughout the ship--each bomb capable of blowing up a battleship. "Sudden death was everywhere, for everyone, for the whole ship; death by fire, explosion, disintegration."

He did not know until later that in the first thirty seconds a wall of fire had swept the entire length of the hangar deck and left in its wake the dead bodies of eight hundred men. Then blast after blast shook the ship as bombs and rockets, shaken free of their moorings, collided with one another and exploded. As they picked their way through the hot wreckage to the upper deck, the men began to panic, crowd up, and become hysterical. O'Callahan's voice snapped them into single file. When they reached the upper decks, the dying were everywhere.

The priest and the Protestant chaplain went from one man to another, prayed with them, and comforted them as best they could. "Their individual religion? Who knows? And who would ask at such a time? . . . The ship trembled as in a mighty earthquake; the noise of the explosions paralyzed my mind. . . . 'Don't be frightened, lad; let's go on with our prayers. Forgive us our trespasses . . . deliver us from evil.'"

As he moved from group to group, he found men unwounded but momentarily paralyzed, not with fear but with awe--the scourging of noise, smoke, and flame was beyond the imagination. The hangar deck was "just one solid mass of fire." All but a hundred feet of the carrier's flight deck was aflame, "not solid fire, as below, but flames, tall as towers, leaping high, snapping in all directions. . . . I know I saw shrapnel, entire airplane engines, shooting through the air. . . . The hundred feet clear was strewn with bodies."

The wounded were in shock and Joe O'Callahan commanded a party of men to search out blankets. He prayed with the

Jewish doctor as his own leg was being bandaged. He joined
a line of men bucking hoses into the flames to reclaim another
hundred feet of the flight deck. He went off to recruit others
to man the hoses. "The men were not following me as much
as they were following the Cross on my helmet. For better or
worse I had become a symbol. My helmet was far more important than my head." And the bombs kept exploding, the
fires raged, and the mangled dying cried for help. It was not
yet nine in the morning.

At nine-thirty the steam failed in the boilers. The screws
stopped turning. The listing Franklin lay dead in the water,
fifty miles offshore and drifting toward Japan.

At ten-fifty the cruiser Santa Fe pulled alongside, tearing
through the overhanging debris of hot steel, shearing off her
own decks. Once locked together with the exploding Franklin,
the fire crews of the cruiser leaped aboard and joined the fire-
fighting while others carried off the wounded from the carrier.
All the pilots were transferred. Joe O'Callahan stayed.

Hundreds of rounds of five-inch shells were stored in the
forward gun turret. If the fires got to them, the ship would
be torn apart. So Joe O'Callahan rounded up a "shell brigade"
to crawl with him into the turret and pass the shells from
hand to blistered hand to be dropped overboard. While they
worked, another crew fought through the smoke to flood the
magazines below decks.

Several times O'Callaghan was called to a telephone connection with men trapped below. "The Captain says he'll get
you out, and he'll get you out. . . . You're better off than
we are. Play acey-deucy and pray."

By sunset the last of the bombs had been dumped. The explosions had ceased. The Franklin was miraculously under
tow. There was now a chance. By 9 a. m. the following morning the engineers had repaired the boilers enough to make
twelve knots on their own power. The towline was cast off.
And then began "the solemn task of burying the dead."

The burials continued all through the day. And then came
the search for undiscovered bodies. "Boys don't like to carry

burned corpses pickaback up steep ladders. I think that I carried most of the corpses. It has been a source of several nightmares since, perhaps because on one trip I was so exhausted that I fell asleep a moment on a step of the ladder. It is disconcerting to awake and find oneself clasping and facing a burned corpse. "

At 10:00 a. m. when the seamen had been sent to catch some sleep, a group of officers joined the priest in burying the last bodies in the sea.

The following day a mimeographed sheet was distributed to the crew headed: "The ship that won't be sunk can't be sunk," and one item read: "Keep busy doing something all the time. If you aren't on a scheduled working party, work anyway. We've got the world by the tail, hang on!"

On April 3, exactly one month after her departure, the Franklin edged into Pearl Harbor with 706 men aboard.

Lieutenant Commander Joseph Timothy O'Callahan, S.J., was the first chaplain ever to receive the Congressional Medal of Honor. But perhaps what meant most to him was hearing that the captain of his ship had said to his mother, "I am not a religious man, but during the height of combat, while I watched your son, I said aloud then, as I say to you now, 'If faith can do that for a man, there must be something to it.'"

Walter Ciszek, 1904-   *Jesuit in Siberia*

BOAC Flight #501 from London was right on time, 6:55 a. m. One of the passengers who came down the ramp was a short, stocky, full-faced man in his late fifties. He wore a green overcoat over a grey suit and dark blue shirt. His face was hidden by a big floppy Russian hat. His name was Walter Ciszek, and he was returning from twenty-seven years inside the Soviet Union, fifteen of them in Siberian prison camps. Years before the members of the New York Province had said the usual two

Masses for the repose of his soul. Walter Ciszek had risen from the dead.

How did he manage to survive? "To me, the answer is simple and I can say quite simply: Divine Providence. . . . I don't just mean that God took care of me. I mean that He called me to, prepared me for, then protected me during those years in Siberia. I am convinced of that; but then, it is my life and I have experienced his hand at every turning."

He had been "born stubborn" in Shenandoah, Pennsylvania, the son of an immigrant coal miner. He was "a bully, a street fighter; . . . and most of the fights I picked on purpose, just for the devilment." His father once took him to the police station and begged them to put him into reform school. In eighth grade Walter made up his mind to be a priest. His father, of course, refused to believe it. But he fooled them all and entered the Polish minor seminary.

"And I had to be tough. I'd get up at four-thirty in the morning to run five miles around the lake on the seminary grounds, or go swimming in November when the lake was little better than frozen. I still couldn't stand to think that anyone could do something I couldn't do, so one year during Lent I ate nothing but bread and water for the full forty days--another year I ate no meat at all for the whole year--just to see if I could do it."

Providence, indeed.

Then Ciszek read the life of St. Stanislaus Kostka, another tough Pole who fought his family and at fourteen walked from Warsaw to Rome to join the Jesuits. Ciszek was three years from ordination. He hated the idea of "perfect obedience." But at age twenty-four without asking anyone's advice he presented himself to the provincial at 501 East Fordham Road in the Bronx and said, "I'm going to be a Jesuit."

On September 7, 1928 he reported to the novitiate in Poughkeepsie, New York. Early in his first year he volunteered to go to Russia and, surprisingly, he was accepted. Only one condition, he had to finish the course of studies first.

At the end of his second year of philosophy, however, he was informed that he was to sail to Rome to begin his theological studies at the Russian College. The only problem was that he couldn't stand the two-hour Russian liturgy! Nonetheless, on June 24, 1937 he was ordained and said his first Mass in the Russian rite.

Since no priest could travel directly into Russia, Ciszek was sent to Albertin, Poland to work for two years teaching ethics to Jesuit seminarians and to be "a horse-and-buggy priest." But on September 1, 1939 Hitler invaded Poland. The novices were sent home. And then the Russians invaded from the east. Ironically, Russia came to him.

The Russians took over the college, threw the books from the library into a dump truck, and left the Jesuits with nothing but the chapel. Then one day Ciszek went into the church to say Mass and found the tabernacle open, the altar cloths strewn about, and the Blessed Sacrament gone. It was the end of the Jesuit mission in Albertin.

Father Ciszek and his inventive friend Father Makar managed to con their way onto one of the jammed trains going south to Lvov, the Jesuit theologate. For awhile Ciszek got a job driving a truck, but the one idea that plagued him was that this was the perfect time for his "invasion" of Russia. The roads were aswarm with refugees. A man could easily lose himself among them. The Russians were hiring large crowds of people to work the factories in the Urals. Finally, his superior said yes.

For the tricky Makar false identity papers were no problem. So Ciszek presented himself at the office of a big lumber combine as "Wladimir Lypinski," a widower whose family had died in a German air raid. On March 15, 1940 he boarded boxcar #89725 with twenty-five other people, an oil-drum stove, a slop bucket for a toilet, and not much else for the fifteen hundred-mile trip to Chusovoy in the Ural Mountains. The trip took two grinding, tedious weeks.

Through the summer of 1940 Walter worked as an unskilled laborer hauling logs from the river and stacking them in long rows on the bank. He was paid by the number of logs stacked, but with old-timers juggling the tallies and lodging deducted from his pay, he was broke within two weeks and had to begin pawning his few possessions to buy food. He had to sneak out into the woods to say Mass. In his spare time he memorized the prayers of the Mass against the time when his Mass kit might be discovered and confiscated. But for the time being his apostolate was loading logs and keeping his ears open.

Then one night early in June at 3 a. m. the barracks were surrounded by secret police. They searched everything. In Ciszek's suitcase they found two bottles of white wine, a can of tooth powder, and some sheets of paper he had used to teach a little boy how to write. The agent claimed they were "bottles of nitrogylcerine, a tin of gunpowder, and a secret code. " Wladimir Lypinski was arrested as a German spy.

For two months he was kept in a cell thirty by thirty feet with about a hundred other prisoners, never the same men, since as new prisoners were shoved in, others were taken out, never to be seen again. Those who did return were battered black and blue.

Finally one day he was called to the interrogation room. "Who are you?" He began the sad story of the widower Lypinski. The interrogator interrupted him: "No, no, no. You are not Lypinski, you are not Russian, and you are not a Pole. You are a priest and your name is Ciszek and you are a spy for the Germans. Now why don't you tell us about it?"

He was stunned. He had no way of knowing how they had found him out. He admitted the story but for an hour uselessly denied that he was a spy for anyone. It was the first of many interrogations. Some were accompanied with rubber clubs. After three months of useless denials, he was shipped to Moscow to one of the most dreaded prisons in the world, Lubianka.

He was put alone into a six by ten foot room whose only window was covered by a sheet of tin. The daily order was always the same: breakfast of bread and hot water; lunch, a dish of water in which fish had been boiled; dinner, three tablespoons of oatmeal. After breakfast he could only think of lunch; after lunch he could only think of dinner. Twice a day he was allowed two minutes in the toilet, watched by a guard. In the door of his room was a peephole so that the guard could roust him to his feet if he lay down during the day. So he paced. And prayed.

After several days he was awakened during the night for interrogation and discovered that the KGB had an astonishing amount of information about his past life. He could not tell where they had gotten it all. He was taken back to his cell and waited for the next interrogation. It didn't come the next day. Or the next. Or the next. The days stretched on into weeks.

So to keep from going stir crazy, he organized his days into a regular order as if he were living in a Jesuit house. "Just as soon as I got up in the morning, I would say the Morning Offering. Then after the morning wash-up I would put in a solid hour of meditation. . . . After breakfast I would say Mass by heart. . . . Before going to bed at night, I'd make the evening examination of conscience and points for the morning meditation, following St. Ignatius' Spiritual Exercises.

"Every afternoon I said three rosaries--one in Polish, one in Latin, and one in Russian--as a substitute for my breviary. After supper I spent the evening reciting prayers and hymns from memory or even chanting them aloud, . . . all the things we had memorized in the novitiate, the hymns we had sung during my years in the Society, the prayers I had learned as a boy at home. . . . I would also recite the poetry I could remember: Wordsworth's 'We Are Seven,' or Shelley's 'Ode to the West Wind,' or Burns' little poem to a field mouse which I found amusingly appropriate in my present condition and which had always been a favorite of mine. Occasionally I'd make up an extemporaneous sermon or speech on some subject, just rambling along, talking aloud in order to keep myself sane."

For three more months he was interrogated every day by the KGB about his alleged subversive activities. Then, since

they could discover nothing but the truth from him, the interrogation was extended another three months. It began all over
again from line one. As the time of the second three-month
period was drawing fruitlessly to an end, they worked him
over for forty-eight hours with drugs and shock treatments.
He had a vague recollection of writing his name. Several
weeks later on July 26, 1942 he was summoned before a commissar at two o'clock in the morning. He had "confessed" and
had been found guilty of espionage. The sentence was fifteen
years at hard labor in Siberia.

He did not know then that it would be four more years before
he left Lubianka.

The next four years he calls his years of education at
"Lubianka University." Besides his previous routine, he did
forty-five minutes of calisthenics every day, polished the floor
twice a day, and sewed his clothes with needles he had made of
fishbones from his soup. Since he had been convicted, the
prison officials allowed him one book at a time and he read
his way through Tolstoy, Dostoevsky, Turgenev, Gogol,
Dickens, Shakespeare, and Goethe--all in Russian. There
were interrogations at irregular intervals, threats, offers of
"deals," but they became little more than irritating interrup-
tions in his hermit's routine.

In May, 1945 the war ended. One year later Walter Ciszek
was finally sent to Siberia.

A year is so much longer when it's spent in one room, alone.
Only after this kind of experience could a man look to Siberia
as something better.

It may be eighteen hundred miles as the crow flies from
Moscow to Krasnoyarsk, halfway across the Russian subcon-
tinent. By train it is twenty-five hundred miles. By boxcar with
thirty men in a car, it takes two weeks.

But Krasnoyarsk was not his destination. Two days after
he had arrived there, he was herded with two thousand other
men onto barges in the Yenisei River for a twenty-day journey
north to Norilsk. When they left Krasnoyarsk, it had been a
sweltering hot day. When they arrived in Norilsk, it was

stinging cold and snowing. They were now ten degrees north of the Arctic Circle.

It was a motley collection of men: thieves, deserters, murderers, political prisoners--and one Vatican spy.

For twelve hours a day in the bitter cold Ciszek shoveled coal into freighters, still dressed in light cotton summer clothes with rags for shoes. Winter clothing was not issued until October when the temperature was thirty degrees below zero.

But for the first time in five years he met another priest and was able to say Mass. Polish prisoners had made wine out of stolen raisins, the paten was a cover for a gold watch, the chalice was a shot glass. "But my joy at being able to celebrate Mass again cannot be described. . . . I heard confessions regularly and from time to time was even able to distribute Communion secretly after I'd said Mass. The experience gave me new strength. I could function as a priest again, and I thanked God daily for the opportunity to work among this hidden flock, consoling and comforting men who had thought themselves beyond His grace. "

Providence, indeed.

In December he was transferred to mining coal, ten hours at a stretch, with no breaks for food or rest. There was no running water in the new camp, so the men simply washed their faces and hands with snow. Everything froze--the food, the dynamite and tools, hands and feet. With the railroad tracks three feet under snow and the river solid with ice, the camp was cut off from all supplies. In the spring thaw, at the end of May, the place was a sea of mud.

Walter Ciszek worked in the mines "about a year," then in 1947 he became a construction worker in an ore processing plant, a better job since there was water to drink and blankets on the beds. Once every ten days, the men got a shower and turned in their old underwear for a clean set. Their other clothes were washed every three months.

After work he heard confessions as the men walked around the prison yard. And once the commandant's quarters had

cleared for the day, he said Mass undetected right in the offices. At times he said Mass in the hospital examination rooms.
He even began giving retreats.

In October, 1953 Ciszek was again sent to work in the mines.
It was bitter cold and the work was brutalizing, but he was
able to make thirty dollars a month which meant he could eat
a little better. He worked in the mines for two more years--
in this story "years" have the danger of looking like "days."
But as his sentence drew agonizingly toward a close, his one
fear was that he would have an accident in the mine within days
of his release.

Finally on April 22, 1955 with three years off for work
quotas surpassed, his sentence was up. He walked out of the
prison a free man. He had survived fifteen years of hell.

His freedom of movement was limited to the town of Norilsk,
so for three years he worked there in a chemical factory.
Most of the girls in the plant knew he was a priest and they
covered for him if he came in late or had to leave early for a
Mass or wedding or baptism. He even made several converts
among them. After awhile he became so busy that he had to
rotate the places for his three Sunday Masses.

One of the first things Ciszek had done when he was released
from the labor camp was to get permission from the secret
police to write to his sisters in America. Suddenly a letter
came. They were astonished that he was alive. For the first
time since 1939, almost twenty years, someone in America
knew that Walter Ciszek was still alive. Twenty years. Twenty
years ago as I type this, I was taking my first vows as a
Jesuit.

By Easter of 1958 there were so many people in Norilsk
for his midnight Mass that there was hardly room in the converted barracks for anyone else. Several men from the secret
police, however, found space.

The following Wednesday he was summoned by the KGB
and given ten days to leave Norilsk "and never think of coming
back." Ten days later a KGB jeep took him to the airport and
put him on a plane to Krasnoyarsk. After twelve years he was

leaving the Arctic. It was a step forward from his harrowing life there. It was a step backward to an unknown city and unknown people. He was fifty-four years old. He had been in Russia since he was thirty-six.

And Walter Ciszek was not a man to stand still.

"By my second month at Krasnoyarsk, I had thriving 'mission' parishes on the Pravi Biereg and in the outskirts and suburbs of the city. One German settlement out beyond the Yenisei Station took over a whole barrack when I said Mass. More than eight hundred people attended, and there were baptisms and marriages before and after Mass sometimes for hours. I served another German community in a kolkhoz farther out and, since I still had my regular parish and the 'missions' on the Right Bank, I had to hold these suburban services on Saturday. . . . I worked sometimes around the clock, getting no sleep at all for more than seventy-two hours. "

Ciszek's light was not easily hidden under a bushel. He was called into the KGB office, his passport was canceled, and he was given forty-eight hours to get out of town.

He got a job as an auto mechanic in Abakan, one hundred miles south of Krasnoyarsk and remained there for four more years. Once again "years" begin to sound like "weeks. " In April of 1963 he received a letter from his sister Helen saying she had finally received a visa to visit Russia in June. The KGB which had denied it over and over again, miraculously gave Ciszek permission to meet his sister in Moscow, but only for twelve days. June came and went. There was a delay in his sister's visa. He waited.

Then, abruptly, in early October he was summoned late at night by the KGB, told to quit his job, and be ready to leave for Moscow in three days. He left the meeting knowing nothing of where he was going or why. The prison camps again? Lubianka? Merely to meet his sisters?

He was met in Moscow by agents of the KGB, taken to a hotel, and for three days, inexplicably, given a VIP tour of the capital. They still refused to answer his questions.

Without warning on October 12, 1963 Ciszek was told to
pack; he was taken to the Moscow airport and introduced to
a man named Kirk from the American consulate. "I couldn't
figure anything out. The KGB agent was nervous. Kirk was
nervous--but about what? Everybody stood around for a moment in silence, as if they were at a wake. Finally, Kuznetsov
said, 'Well, shall we get it over with?'
   "'Good,' said Kirk, 'let's get it over with.' The two of them
shook hands, then Mr. Kirk turned to me. 'Father Ciszek,
would you come over here?' I went over to the table as Mr.
Kirk pulled a paper from his inside coat pocket. 'Would you
sign this?' He handed me a pen and I signed; I was so badly
confused I hadn't even the sense to notice what I was signing.
   "'Now, Father Ciszek,' said Mr. Kirk, 'you're an American citizen.'
   "'Really?' I asked, momentarily stunned. 'It's all like a
fairy tale,' I mumbled.
   "'Yes, it's a fairy tale, but a fine fairy tale. And it's true.'"
   Even at that moment, he had no idea that he was to be exchanged for a Russian spy apprehended in the United States.
Numbly he boarded the plane. "Suddenly, the plane gathered
speed. I blessed myself, then turned to the window as we took
off. The plane swung up in a big circle; there were the spires
of the Kremlin in the distance! Slowly, carefully, I made the
sign of the cross over the land I was leaving."

Pierre Teilhard de Chardin, 1881-1955   *Cosmic Adventurer*

As an old man of sixty-nine, learned and famous the world
over, Teilhard de Chardin wrote, "I was certainly no more
than six or seven when I began to feel myself drawn by Mat-
ter--or more exactly by something that 'shone' at the heart of
Matter." For him the scientist, as for Hopkins the poet, the
material world was endlessly rich, endlessly absorbing because of the God who is the "freshness deep-down things."

So at the end of his high school years when it came time to choose between being a scientist or a priest, between Matter and God, he chose them both.

Because of the French government's hostility to the Society, the Jesuit scholasticate had been moved from Aix-en-Provence to the island of Jersey, and there Teilhard suffered his first great crisis as a Jesuit. In his fervor for supernatural realities his attraction to natural science seemed, in contrast, worldly, heavy, unbecoming for a man of God. "I was saved from going off the rails at this moment by the robust good sense of my Master of Novices. In fact he assured me that the God of the Cross expected the natural expansion of my being just as much as its sanctification--without explaining to me how or why."

From then on it was the ideal and task of his life to explain how and why these two loves, science and religion, were not antagonistic but organic parts of the same dynamic thrust toward the fulfillment of the universe. In burrowing deeper into the secrets of Matter, he was burrowing closer to the secrets of God.

His first steps were in the direction of geology and geography. It was only little by little that he came to paleontology and prehistory. Teilhard had made natural science collections as a boy, done some field work at Jersey, but in 1905 when he was sent by his superiors to teach physics in Cairo he became fascinated with the ways in which the stratifications of rock could reveal the history of the earth and of men. He began to sense the evolution of matter and the presence of the creative God within matter, urging it toward fulfillment.

He finished his theology at Hastings in England, was ordained in 1912, and began special studies at the Museum of Natural History in Paris.

In 1914, however, World War I erupted in Europe. All able men were pressed into service, and Teilhard, who had done a year of military service during his Jesuit training, signed up again, not as a chaplain but as a stretcher-bearer. He did

101

not want to be a priest-officer but, as he says, "a priest-comrade to whom a man can turn when things go wrong. "

He felt, first of all, that service was unavoidable, but his volunteering also had a bit of adventure in it, a spirit he followed again and again in his life. "So far as I can remember, I have always lived in a forward-looking tension. " Whenever he felt that tension slacken, he became uneasy. There was always something more to be achieved. He had to be in a state of perpetual "newness. " As a scientist and philosopher he felt a constant drive to get a firmer grip on the truths he'd discovered, to say it more clearly, more accurately. "Don't you believe it's a matter of loyalty and conscience to strive to extract from the world all that this world can hold of truth and energy?"

As a priest the spirit of adventure drew him where the best men of his generation were, to the trenches. After his sheltered seminary days, this was an eye-opener. He was confronted, savagely, with the reality of death: "I ought to be happy every morning at thinking that I have a chance sometime during the day of appearing before Our Lord and finally possessing him. . . . Separations are the price we must pay for Our Lord's entering into us a little further. "

But the trenches were also a confrontation with the very palpable cruelty of man for man, even on the same side. "I am greatly struck by this double fact: the very small number of souls in whom the need for religion has awoken, and the extraordinary vulgarity that goes with this deadness. The Christian souls in my circle are very few in number, but it is as clear as daylight that they are, with rare exceptions, the only ones that are 'fulfilled,' the only ones that are truly human. And so the apparent failure of religion is in reality a triumphant vindication of the need of it and of its effectiveness. May I confess, just to your ears, that at times I feel terribly tired of the selfish bourgeois (to put it no worse) surroundings I am imprisoned in? At such moments I long to dismiss all this world to its bottles or its bunk and build myself an ivory tower. But, from the Christian angle, that would be shameful. Did our Lord do anything but step down and teach us? I must remain on good terms with the 'common herd' and keep contact with it. Pray that God may help me to do so. "

Just as the Spirit of God works its way through the resistance of matter to transform it, so the Spirit of God works its way through the brutal inner resistance of human beings to transform them, and assisting that birth is the task of the priest.

And Teilhard did his job with a will. After four years at the front, he was given the Croix de Guerre, the military medal, and the Legion of Honor. While machine guns were still sweeping the ground, he would dash out close to the enemy lines, find a wounded man, pick him up on his back, and crawl to the rear. The men in his platoon complained that he did too much. The victims were often dead anyway.

The men frequently saw that he was "busy inside. " He was indeed, busy with the dazzling Presence running through all creation. "More than ever I believe life is beautiful; even in the grimmest circumstances, when you look around, God is there. " It is astonishing how many letters and articles he managed to write even with shells bursting all around him. He had a kind of prophetic impatience, something he had to share because at any moment death might silence him.

After demobilization in 1919 Teilhard returned to the paleontology laboratory of the Paris Museum and prepared his doctoral dissertation, a study of the first mammals. After defending the dissertation, he accepted a professorship in geology at the Institut Catholique in Paris which he held for four years. However, in 1923 he received an invitation to come to China from a fellow Jesuit, Pere Licent, who had created a laboratory and museum for geological and paleontological research there. His provincial approved and he was off in pursuit of another adventure. "I was caught. The enigmatic and tiresome 'I' who so . . . loves the front line is exactly the same person . . . who loves adventure and research, who always wants to go off to the far ends of the world to have new and unusual experiences and to be able to say he is ahead of everyone. "

As he hammered at stones near Tientsin and crated up fossils of prehistoric hyenas, gazelles, and bison, his letters reflect his meditations on the Aliveness that had worked itself out and left these fossils as the footprints of his passing. "As I pray, I gradually work out a bit better my 'Mass upon Things.' It seems to me that in a sense the true elements that have to be consecrated every day are the growth of the world that day: the bread symbolizing appropriately what Creation manages to produce, the wine (blood) what it loses through exhaustion and suffering in its labor. . . . For, as you know, I only came to China in the hope of being better able to speak of 'the mighty Christ' in Paris. Indeed, I feel more and more strongly that it is only this 'mighty Christ' who can animate all my life."

In September of 1924 he returned to France and began to lecture and write articles on the vision he saw of the Divine Presence in the evolutionary movement of creation. "I am so fully and so rationally convinced of the spiritual value of the urge toward consciousness, the very sap of the tree of life of which our privileged species occupies the summit."

Criticism was not slow in coming, nor has it ended yet. Scientists balked at his poetic language. Theologians began to wonder if he was not becoming pantheistic, making the unchangeable God into a growing part of the evolutionary process. His superiors began to get nervous. Although he was never condemned, he was warned by Rome to confine his published work to science. It was a heartbreaking blow to him and, although he bowed with a truly holy obedience, he said that the struggle to submit gave him the feeling of "growing old."

He turned back, then, to China. "Here are the Indies which draw me more than those which drew St. Francis Xavier. But here too are enormous problems, not of rites but of ideas, to be resolved before we can truly convert them." He saw that if men and women would only forget themselves "as Chinese or French and see themselves as fellow Terrestrials," there would be hope.

This was precisely the liberating, supranational vision Matteo Ricci had had 350 years before. Like Ricci, Teilhard forged his authority as a scientist only to assure his claims as a priest. Like Ricci, Teilhard "went over to the Chinese," adopting their ways so that their fear of foreigners would not be an obstacle to the message of Christianity. Like Ricci, he worked in Peking.

In March, 1927 Teilhard completed what he called "my devotional book," The Divine Milieu. It is a hymn to the omnipresence of God in the universe. In the Epistle to the Colossians St. Paul had seen Christ as "the bodying-forth of the invisible God . . . all things are created in him and for him. And he is before all things, and by him all things consist." To Teilhard, all that we see--even Matter itself--is somehow a physicalization of the aliveness of Christ urging the universe to its fulfillment. In that sense matter itself is "holy."

All the potential in matter and man is waiting for divinization by God, and the priest is God's agent in bringing that about. As he says in his book on the priesthood, "To the full extent of my power, because I am a priest, I wish from now on to be the first to become conscious of all that the world loves, pursues and suffers; I want to be the first to seek, to sympathize, and to suffer; the first to unfold and sacrifice myself--to become more widely human and more nobly of the earth than any of the world's servants."

He sent The Divine Milieu in mimeographed form to his friends but, like all his philosophical works, it remained in that form until after his death.

At that time he accepted an offer from the Carnegie Foundation to supervise work on the study of vertebrate fossils and the origin of man in China. This was the expedition which unearthed the remnants of Sinanthropus, the so-called "Peking Man": jawbones and fragments of skull of a very strange anthropoid or humanoid; the teeth are entirely human (but) the shape of the jaw is typically ape-like; cranium of quite human dimensions (?)" What was more, the bones were found with what looked like primitive tools.

It seemed that his party had found at least a missing link tying man to an ape-ancestor. The theological problem was obvious: both Hebrews and Christians maintained that even with evolution, humanity--the ability to think and reflect--was given in a single act, not in a gradual process of increasing immaterial thought out of a previously thoughtless material body. Otherwise a material cause would be generating an immaterial effect, which it had no power to do. And yet, physically, Sinanthropus seemed part ape, part man.

Teilhard faces that question: "This is the moment to insist that no consideration drawn from paleontology can ever detract from the astonishing grandeur of the present human fact. Human paleontology labors only, in fact, to discover the embryogenesis of the human species. But embryonic states cannot enable one to define the value of the adult-being in the case of Man-as-species any more than in the case of Man-as-individual. "

He is saying, in effect, that no one could look at an acorn, or a small pile of paleolithic bones, or a human embryo and make any accurate guess about the shape of the oak, about modern man as we know him, or about which embryo will create "Hamlet" and which will create an atom bomb.

The death of his father far away in France and the death of his colleague Davidson Black in Peking had a profound effect on Teilhard. "What an absurd thing life is, on the surface. . . . So absurd that one is thrown back upon a stubborn and desperate faith in the reality and survival of the Spirit. Otherwise-- I mean, if there is no such thing as Spirit--we would be imbeciles not to go on strike against all human effort. . . . In the disorganization that followed Black's death, and in the oppressive atmosphere of 'agnostic' condolences which surrounded it, I took an oath, on the body of my dead friend, to struggle harder than ever to give hope to man's labor and research. "

After trips to Africa, India, and Java, he found that at fifty he was growing tired, too easily exhausted to endure "long journeys by mule, dirty inns, flies," and the harrowing effort of probing mounds of rock all day with a hammer. Moreover, the past had already yielded up its evidence. In it he had seen the springs of aliveness and Mind as they began to emerge. "And preoccupation with the future tends to sweep

everything else aside. . . . Now that the fundamental discovery has been made, namely that we are borne on by an ad-
vancing wave of consciousness, what is there left of importance to discover behind us?"

He felt, too, that he was now one of the world's few authorities in prehistory and his credentials as a scientist were unshakable. It was time now to collect and form his spiritual
testament, a work showing the complete interpenetration of
Mind and Matter, not only in man but in the whole universe. It
would be his apostolic Epistle to Scientists. All his expedi-
tions and research had been nothing more to him than what
he calls a "platform." "My science, to which I owe so much,
seems to me less and less sufficient as an aim in itself. The
true interest in my life has for a long time lain in an effort
more fully to find God in the world. It's a more tricky subject, but it's the only vocation I can recognize, and nothing
will make me deviate from it."

There had been a few first-runs at the final work, essays
like "The Structuring of the Spirit," "The Spirit of the Earth,"
"Why and How I Believe"--each one a further refinement,
each one an attempt to put the hugeness of his vision into
words people would understand as he intended them. Much of
what he wrote was intended for circulation only among professional friends, not merely because of the stricture from Rome
but because he himself saw that only professionals could grapple with the intricacies of his thought without becoming confused or even scandalized.

All that he needed in order to write the great synthesis of
his thoughts was the leisure to do it, and providence, through
the Second World War, immobilized him in Peking from June
1938 to June 1940. It was then that he wrote The Phenomenon
of Man.

This is not the place for an explanation of a work which
experts are still analyzing, and which I myself can make no
pretense to understand beyond the surface. It is filled with so
many unusual and newly coined terms that the reader might
be mind-boggled. Teilhard himself says in his preface that

this is a book by a scientist for scientists to lead them through science to the Source of life. What follows is merely a primer.

It had already been commonplace to see man as a microcosm, a summary of the universe. In the brief nine months of his gestation, each human fetus repeats the physical steps of evolution: cell to growth to movement to sensitive life. But by its very nature, life ascends; it does not remain on the same level. Teilhard's thesis is that evolution does not stop at birth but surges on upward from sensitive life to intelligent life to divine life. Christianity, then, is the ultimate natural step in the evolution of the universe.

Thus man is not just one different species among the other animals. Animals may have consciousness, too, but man has "consciousness squared." With the appearance of man "the Earth . . . discovers its soul." With the appearance of Jesus Christ, man--the peak of evolution so far--opens out into the aliveness of God.

If this is true, Teilhard says, "there is less difference than one might think between Research and Adoration." The property of attraction within particles of matter which brings them into molecular union, and the attraction of persons which forms families and nations and the ultimate human brotherhood are similar manifestations of the Love-Energy who began the universe from outside Time and Space, who impels all creation upward toward the Omega Point, a fulfillment who is Christ.

Teilhard can be criticized on scientific and on philosophical grounds. I leave this to the experts. But in passages which are more accessible to the average reader, he seems to be incurably, and perhaps unjustifiably, optimistic in the face of Dachau, overpopulation, ecological suicide, and atomic cataclysm. In his enthusiasm for the surge of aliveness, he becomes at times rhapsodic, lost in poetic statement, and thus unclear.

But in the face of our anguish, as science expands the known universe and we seem consequently so tiny as to be meaningless, Teilhard gives hope to men that a man's physical smallness has nothing to do with his immortal importance. This, I think, is also the message of Jesus Christ.

Many will ask how a modern man can still remain or become a Jesuit. The reply to such a question can only be the very personal one of each Jesuit. . . .

And so for me, in the final analysis, it is no great matter what credit the Society has in the history of culture or of the Church, what credit goes to a line of men with a spirit like that, nor does it matter to me if a similar spirit is found in other groups, named or nameless.

The fact is that the spirit exists here. I think of brothers that I myself have known--of my friend Alfred Delp who with hands chained signed his declaration of final membership in the Society; of one who in a village in India that is unknown to Indian intellectuals helps poor people to dig their wells; of another who for long hours in the confessional listens to the pain and torment of unimportant people who are far more complex than they appear on the surface . . . of one who assists daily in the hospital at the bedside of death until that unique event becomes for him a dull routine. . . . And so for those who live within the Society its future becomes, after all, a thing of secondary importance, and for that reason its future remains full of hope.

Karl Rahner, S.J.

The Unknown 4

Shifting Gears

Every man in the Society is not a Francis Xavier. We also have
men who don't work enough and those who drink too much. We
have men who find their personal apostolates more important
than loyalty to their brothers. We have men who have forgotten
the freedom of the Exercises. If life in the Society were uniformly perfect, every Catholic male in the world would be
lined up at the novitiate doors.

But both the heroes and the helpless are few. The rest of
the spectrum is made up of men, perhaps one hundred thousand
in the last 450 years, who have worked from dawn through
dark in anonymous generosity. They have graded vocabulary
quizzes, sat in confessionals, changed altar linens, and offered Mass in barrios and parishes and high schools and colleges and seminaries and retreat houses all over the globe.
They have endured their own shortcomings and their brothers' shortcomings, offered their little heroisms to the peo-

ple they served, and grown to know and love Jesus Christ each in his own unheralded way.

I have devoted nearly a half of this book to about a dozen Jesuits whose names have become bywords to their brothers. But they are only a small fraction of the Society of Jesus. How much space could I give to the vast majority of Jesuits who will never have their names in a newspaper, and yet who have been and are the Society of Jesus of which the dozen heroes rejoiced to be a part? It is, after all, this majority that a young Jesuit will join.

The only way I can try to give even a small notion of what the ordinary men of the Society are like is to talk of the ones I know and have known. Thus we'll have a shift of gears here from the indisputably heroic to the disputably ordinary.

I have also spoken up to now about what some men did with their vocations but very little about how each man got his vocation. It is easier to talk about the fruits of a vocation than about how it was planted, how it first broke through, how it was nurtured. The achievements of a man's Jesuit life are a matter of public record, while the first feelings of being "called" are something a man wrestles with for months in the depths of his soul and which surface perhaps only a few times with a confessor or advisor.

I could, to coin a phrase, kill two birds with one stone if I spoke of the origins and growth of one vocation and of the contemporary Jesuits who helped it to grow.

The only vocation I know from the inside, from its first moments until now is my own. I can remember its first unwelcome stirrings, the steps I took to abort it or at least dodge it, the moment of recognition that it was unavoidable, the exhilaration of finally saying "yes," and the months of wondering whether "no" might have been far better.

And just as clearly I can remember so many of my "unknown" brothers from 1951 until now who have helped me shape my vocation, which is now the same as myself. They lived with me, learned with me, suffered with me. Older Jesuits shared their vocations with me in formal lectures as

I sat in their classrooms, and with advice as I sat in their offices or knelt at their prie-dieus. Young Jesuits, "the men around my time," have given a particular form to my Jesuit life: I have seen them working; I have seen some leave; I have seen some grow old; I have seen some die. The "brains" in my year have made me grow, but so have the men who failed. I have learned from watching saints, but I have also learned from watching drunks, and I have become less and less sure that the two are mutually exclusive. All the Jesuits I have known have added something to the Jesuit I have become.

The danger of speaking of my own vocation and of the men who made it grow is that it will appear to be a "model" vocation, a template against which a man can judge whether he has a vocation himself. That would be absurd. The great difference of form in which the calls came and grew in the men already described in this book is ample proof of that. But some elements in all vocations are the same: the Caller, the need to serve, the willingness to give up everything and start over, a measure of guts and a measure of "smarts," and a need to love more than a handful of people.

I wish I could offer a more objective case. But this is the only vocation I know from the inside, the only one I know all about. Well, almost all about.

One last caution. Even if I speak of my own vocation and of the "unknown" Jesuits I have known, remember that mine is a story of a call heard twenty-five years ago. My vocation grew in a course of studies which has changed quite a bit. My vocation was enriched by different men from those a new candidate will meet today.

But it's the best I can do.

For the specific questions of how a vocation will actually grow in the 70's and what the Jesuit of the future will actually be, I can only give the answer our Lord gave to the same questions: "Come and see."

On the surface, the world in which my vocation and I grew up
might seem as remote as the castle of Loyola or the courts
of Peking. Except in science fiction, there were no TVs, no
automatic appliances, no trips to the moon. There was no
atom bomb. We were just crawling out from under the Depres-
sion and, I'm told, my mother and dad ate Wheaties three
times a day so that my sister and I could have meat.

But it wasn't as much like a Dickens novel as it sounds.
Nor was it--under the surface differences--that much different from growing up today or growing up in Renaissance Spain
or growing up in Roman-occupied Judaea. All of us were al-
ternately shy and swaggering, wore the same masks to cover
our ignorance and our fears, craved the understanding of our
parents and our peers. We all feared loneliness.

We were torn by the same contradictory tension between
selfishness and generosity: we wanted the palazzo in Beverly
Hills surrounded by warm-eyed blondes, and at the same
time we wanted a hut in China surrounded by a swarm of
lepers. To be perfectly frank though, I suspect we were not
as sophisticated nor as self-aware as young men are today.
Adolescence as a stage was not really "invented" and studied
and exploited and shouted until after World War II. In fact
even today, the United States is about the only place it has
the leisure to exist. Life was less complicated then and so,
I suppose, were we. But finding oneself, whether as a lawyer
or a priest or a soldier, whether in the 50's, the 70's, or
the 90's, never was and never will be easy.

My parents, like most parents, were good people whose
greatness I, like most kids, never realized until I was much
older. It does give me some pride though, that I had the
courage to blow my cool and tell them how precious they were
to me before it was too late. They said their prayers without
ostentation or shame, went to Mass and novenas and missions,
worked without thanks for lawn fetes and bazaars and all the

other genial extortions that keep Catholic schools afloat. Like all good listeners to Father Coughlin, their statements about Jews and "the colored" would have curled your hair, but their treatment of them would have warmed your heart.

And they loved my sister and me and one another in the only way they knew how to: they worked. God, how they worked! Which, I have no doubt, is why I have more respect for a single dollar than for a thousand dollars and why my own attitude toward work would gladden the heart of the flintiest commissar. Yet it was someone as unworldly as Kahlil Gibran who said, "Work is love made visible."

Naturally, I was ashamed of my parents. It was ugly, now that I look back on it, but when I look at all the other kids I knew and know, it seems at least "usual" if not natural. My friends' parents were always more glamorous, richer, better conversationalists, better-educated, broader-minded, sophisticated. And little prig that I was, it was a shamingly long time before I realized I had been living with something far more important: two honest-to-God saints.

It is a cliche to speak this way when talking about vocations, but I can't avoid it: if it were not for my parents, I'm sure I'd be out there in Competitionville with a $50,000 job and a pair of ulcers. Instead I became a priest in great part because my parents proved to me that counting money is not as important as loving people.

Even in first grade I was a canny little cuss. Whenever Sister Mary Cecilia told us to write a composition on What-I-Want-to-Be-When-I-Grow-Up, I was always shrewd enough to know what answer got an A: "I want to be a preest, Sister!" How was I to know I was going to get caught at it, and she'd be at my ordination?

The odd thing is that I also said I was going to be a Jesuit. I don't remember ever meeting one or even reading about them, but I always said "Jesuit." Perhaps it was the fact that Jimmy Belzer said he was going to be a Columban and Richie McNamara said he was going to be a Franciscan, and I didn't want to risk a B+ by being "usual." Or perhaps it was just that Somebody Else wanted it that way.

I was, to my utter disgrace, a "brain"--the cause being that I was certain I wouldn't be loved if I failed. So I worked my tiny tail off. What was worse, I wasn't even the best brain. I was always beaten in those innocence-destroying competitions by Jane White who, it so happened, was a girl. What was worst, Jane White could also play basketball, football, baseball, and even dodgeball better than I could! Let it be known that I was and am, notoriously and irrevocably, the most inept unjock in all Christendom. That disgrace was coupled with the onslaught of acne in-eighth grade, a case which lasted so long into high school that I thought it would be terminal. The combination almost made me up the ante and tell the eighth grade nun I'd be a Trappist. That would have been good for an A+.

What I also got in eighth grade was an insatiable appetite for books. One of my greatest achievements that year, while my apple-cheeked peers were battering hell out of a football and one another, was reading two complete and unabridged Tarzan books in one Saturday afternoon. Doubtless part of the impetus was the scorchy relationship hinted at between Tarzan and Jane, but most of it came from Sister Mary Denis who had turned me into a book junkie. It is a gift I can never pay for and one for which, shamefully, I have never thanked her.

One of my rare demonstrations of spine in those early years was my devious resistance to piano lessons. It pains me still to remember my mother hauling me by the ear, literally, across the seats and up the aisle of the Saturday serial in the Kenmore Theater and back to Mrs. Stearns' house for a piano lesson. I saw a lot of movies; in fact I logged most of my transitional hours in the Colvin Theater around the corner. But my rebellion against the piano still angers me and shows once again that Ma was wiser than I.

My mother was a tough lady. Besides piano lessons she suggested on pain of starvation that I get a paper route and (gasp!) take dancing lessons. With a woman oblivious to irate theater ushers and audiences, the outcome was beyond resistance or dispute. But the paper route netted me some eighteen dollars a week, gave me spending money and tuition and independence and the first faint suspicions of selfhood. The dancing lessons gave me girls. Good ol' Ma!

When I tell people I now know that I was shy as a kid, they laugh themselves into cardiac arrest. But I was. And my shyness with girls was nearly catatonic. Part of it was the ignominious encounters I had had with Jane White in the groves of academe and on the blacktop arenas of St. John the Baptist Grammar School. Part of it was also a lethal dosage of Puritanism and a cosmic sexual ignorance: I was convinced that if I touched a girl above the wrist her father had every right to come after me with a shotgun in one hand and a birth certificate in the other. But my shyness was mostly due to the feeling every boy has beneath his bravado that girls are scary and dangerous because they have the greatest power in the world, the power to turn you down, which to a young kid is equivalent to annihilation.

My years in the darkness of the Kenmore and Colvin Theaters coincided with the mystic eruption of puberty and as Rita Hayworth slowly peeled off that one black satin opera glove in "Gilda," I dissolved in innocent lust. All three nights. But the screen was one step removed from reality. When my palpitating heart shuddered back to normal, I admitted with relief that old Rita was just a harmless pattern of light and shadow on a screen. Rita would never reject me. Rita would never say, the way a real girl could, "Get lost, creep!"

At her dance classes every Saturday night Miss Elias provided the real thing. First of all, Miss Elias was every inch a lady, warm, elegant, lovely; and I had a long-distance crush on her for two years. But more important, when the combo started and Miss Elias chanted "one, two, and step-close," there was no avoiding it; ol'Bill had to take a girl right into his arms.

I loved it. To speak truth, I still love it. And for the first time I got to know girls not as relatives or competition or threats to my priceless virtue, but as people. And I owe a great deal of growing up to Nancy Atkinson and Marilyn Connors and Susie Deckop and Margy Brown. Especially Marge.

But it surely put any thoughts of being a priest into cold storage!

Nonetheless something was happening underground. When I had graduated from grade school, I knew more certainly than ever that I was going to Canisius High, because Jesuits taught there. I had finished seventh in the scholarship exam for the Christian Brothers' school. There were, of course, only six scholarships given. But even if all six ahead of me reneged, I had made up my mind I wouldn't take that scholarship. Of course it was insane; my family hadn't a farthing; the scholarship would have meant at least three months' salary to my Dad or ten months' salary to me. But still I would have turned it down. I didn't have the slightest notion or question why going to Canisius meant so much, but I remember telling my Dad, who was a quiet undemonstrative man, that come hell or high water or scholarship, I was going to Canisius. He just nodded and said, "If that's what you want." I never thanked him for that.

At Canisius I met some of the finest men I've ever known: shy, kindly men like Jacksie Boyle, hotshots like Paul Curtin, whip-crackers like John Paone, warm and genial natural-born teachers like Tom McMahon, plus a few men who could put a volcano to sleep.

The appeal these men had for me was not as religious or as priests, but as men. They seemed to walk in an aura of confidence. They knew who they were and where they were going. They were genuine, warm, knowledgeable, unafraid to kid one another even in front of us. I was amazed that even when one of them had indisputably flubbed, the others stuck up for him, sometimes fiercely. They were men. The kind of men I, or any kid, would want to be. And there was a bit of mystery about them too, something elusive, something they had with one another that we couldn't share no matter how close we got to them. One morning I found out what it was.

I usually got to school early. One reason was that I got up early for my paper route. Another was that I usually hit Mass at Canisius before class. But the real reason was that I loved the place. One morning, it must have been December 8, I got to school and went to the chapel but, strangely, there was a Mass already going on. The door was open and I stood back where I wouldn't be seen. As the time for communion came, the rector turned with the ciborium and a host in his hand and one by one the scholastics came up, knelt at his feet, and recited some prayer in Latin. They were renewing their vows as Jesuits. Without being told I began to suspect that this was part of what they had with one another that we couldn't share.

By senior year I was practically a walking vocation poster. I gag to recall it; but I was a good kid, wisecracking within acceptable limits most of the time, unafraid anymore of girls, smart, hard-working, generous, a writer and an actor and-- though sickeningly unathletic--a prime target for the vocation hook.

And, boy, did I get it!

Most of the Jesuits I knew well contented themselves with very indirect verbal nudges. But one day during Easter vacation I was working alone in the yearbook office. One of the scholastics came in and sat down; and even though I had a lot of work to do, I felt warm and flattered that he liked me and wanted to talk to me. But he was so studiedly nonchalant that I could see the curve ball coming even before he wound up. It was the old vocation pitch.

Well, it lasted for two hours; and the more he talked, the more my mind closed. I sure as hell wasn't as certain about my "call" as he seemed to be. I still had to test myself. I wanted to write and act. There were a lot more girls out there, too many challenges yet for me to lock myself up in some seminary. Even the word sounded like "cemetery"! This is one reason why most Jesuits and I hesitate to come right out and ask a man if he wants to talk about a Jesuit vocation. Right then and there I was on my way to Holy Cross College and, I thought, on my way away from the Jesuit novitiate.

Holy Cross was good for me. At the time it wasn't the Athens of the West or anything. In fact the only superlative teacher I had there was Harry Bean, a crusty old priest who taught English and Latin rhetoric and made me conscious for the first time of structure in prose and the tricks of speech that make dull prose come alive.

What I did find at Holy Cross was resilience and wit and the first beginnings of a self-trust that has since grown into nearly Kamikaze aggressiveness. When I went there I was far too naive, far too sensitive. I suspect it was only by my sophomore year in college that I acquired the toughness of skin that most high school seniors today consider an automatic part of their defense equipment. I owe that toughness to Harry Bean and Jack Coyle, but mostly to Don Matthews, who resisted the call two years longer than I did.

At Holy Cross I always had a confessor and usually kicked things around with him once every week or two. I chose Paddy Cummings not because I found him particularly appealing but because Frank Hart, the student counselor, was so holy I was afraid I'd shock him and because Luke O'Connor had the reputation of being on the prowl for Jesuit recruits. The major reason I chose Paddy, I guess, was that he was "in." All my newfound jock friends swore he was a Solomon come amongst us again. Even though I didn't see it, I kept going every week or so. I didn't realize at the time that the problem wasn't with Paddy's Solomonic powers but with me. I didn't need the wisdom of the ages to solve my simple problems.

And then I did.

By November of sophomore year I hadn't yet seen Paddy since school began. The principal reason was that it had been a somewhat "heavy" summer. Not that it was ravaging my soul or even that it was in the forefront of my mind. I was just getting along without too much confession.

Then one night as I sat in my room trying to study, it was as if the black dog were on my back. Nobody had said anything crucifying to me; nobody had done anything. It was just there. I felt oppressed, ugly, miserable. Without a word to my roommates, I just set my jaw, stalked out the door, and started walking up the hill behind the college. It was a clear, star-crowded night, and I was wretched. And the worst part was that I had no inkling why I should be so wretched. It was like being detested, leprous, contemptible; and yet I knew, helplessly, that no one felt that way about me or had reason to. It had nothing to do with the summer. It was just there, ugly, unconnected with anything.

How long I was up on the hill, I don't know; but I know that for no apparent reason at all I broke into great racking sobs. And although it sounds stupidly dramatic now, I remember shaking my fist at the sky and saying, "Goddamit! If there's something I've got to do, what is it!" And then I went down and sat in the balcony of the Jesuits' chapel and sobbed some more.

I think it was a week or two later that I fell into step with Paddy Cummings as he was walking on the hill reading his breviary. I went to confession, told him the whole thing, and without any comments or sermons, he gave me absolution. Then, out of a clear sky, I said, "Okay. If they'll still take me, I'll go. "

"Huh? Go where?"

"Into the Jesuits. "

"You never said anything about that before. "

And I hadn't. No stretch of the imagination could have called it a "decision. " I hadn't planned it or worked it out. It wasn't in any sense to "pay" for my scarlet sins. It had no connection in my mind with anything. It was just there. And I knew-- illogically, unreasonably, undeniably--that it was right.

As the weeks passed, the more Paddy and I hashed it out carefully and soberly, the "right-er" it became.

It began to look like a conspiracy.

After the Decision

The only thing wrong about the decision was that I knew for sure that they were going to turn me down. So with more good luck than wisdom, I told no one except Paddy; not my roommates, not even my parents. I filled out the forms, had a physical, saw the three examiners at Holy Cross, who, I suspected, wouldn't have known me before or after if they had found me dead in their johns.

Then I had to take the test in New York. That's when I was going to be exposed as the fraudulent weakling I knew I was. I told my roommates I was going to New York for a cousin's wedding. I didn't have a cousin within five hundred miles of New York. As I rode the train, the wheels kept clicking-- honest t'God--"It's the right thing, the right thing, the right thing." And my head kept clanging, "Wrong!"

I stayed at Fordham for three days for no other reason than to substantiate the cousin's wedding story. As I sweated over the test, a boy next to me said, "What the hell are you so nervous about?" I told him I was afraid they'd turn me down. He almost sneered, "They don't turn anybody down." I never saw him again.

On the way back to Worcester I stopped in the Grand Central Station Flower Shoppe and bought a white carnation. When I got back, I threw it on Don Matthews' desk and said, cool as wintergreen, "Souvenir of the wedding." I actually did that! Gasp.

I had a meeting with the dean, Father Fitzgerald, and told him in passing about my "subterfuges." He wondered a bit about my lying so much and so professionally. But I said that it was self-defense against the inevitable.

And I waited.

Then one day in spring I got a call to Fitz's office. Dread. I went in and he said with disarming gentleness, "WELL! You want them to think we're damn fools down there in New York?"

Answer that one.

I told him I didn't know what he meant, and he said with the same gut-melting growl, "You didn't send them your baptismal certificate. " It didn't even seem stupid to me, and I leaped to my feet and said I'd call my parents and tell them to send it air mail special delivery.

"SIT DOWN!" he averred.

I sat. Trembling.

"I don't know why I get these dirty jobs, " he snarled.

I shook.

"We did get final word on you today. "

"Which way did it go?" My legs were spaghetti.

"Which way do you think?"

By that time I was damn near in tears.

"You're supposed to report to St. Andrew-on-Hudson on July 30th. "

Silence. No breath.

"God! Why did you do that to me?"

"Well, I figured that a future priest had deceived so many people for so long that he ought to get a little of his own back. "

I thanked Fitz, breathless, and dashed out of the office and whooped up the hundreds of steps of the library up to our dorm, burst into the room and shouted, "Guess what!"

Matthews looked up from his book and said, "You're going into the Jesuits. " I could have killed him.

Only slightly deflated, I ran to the phone and called home, collect. When I told my mother, she said, "Dad and I thought you were going to do that. "

So much for my unparalleled skill as a secret agent.

But it was done. I'd said yes, and they'd said yes, and I was in.

After I was accepted some wise old Jesuit told me, "Don't become a novice till you get in the front door. " And I didn't. There were dates, parties, minor indiscretions, and I drank rather more beer than a prudent man ought.

Still there were questions that kept catching me unaware, especially when I was having fun: how can I do that for the rest of my life? Why a priest? Other men lead good lives as married laymen. Why a religious? Diocesans do a lot of work for the Church. The one question that never came up was why a Jesuit. That had been emerging more and more clearly since I was a kid in first grade. Whatever the Jesuits I knew "had," I wanted that. No matter what happened it was worth an honest try; and I remember telling my Dad when I left that if I were home within a year, he'd know they'd thrown me out.

On the 28th of July, 1951 I took a plane to New York, met two Holy Cross friends who were also entering, cavorted on the beach, went to the racetrack for the first and last time in my life, fell in love with one of my friend's sisters, and two days later, on July 30th, the three of us drove into the grounds of St. Andrew-on-Hudson.

The first novice we met was Jerry McMahon. As we were parking the car, he ran up in a ratty old army surplus jacket with a rake in his hand. "Hi, I'm Brother Manuductor." And he showed us the way to the front door. I can remember saying to myself, "That guy sure has an Irish-looking face for such a Greek name."

Dick Noonan opened the front door for us, welcomed us, and as he opened the door to the novitiate, said, "Of course, you know we're on silence in the house."

It would have been gentler to use a sledge hammer.

For the rest of the day we were outfitted in black jackets some old Jesuits had died in, large jackets for the shrimps, tiny jackets for the giants. Everywhere we went we traveled in godawful lugubrious lines, even to the bathrooms. We toured the house, played the first of what would prove to be an endless series of softball games (take that, Jane White!), went to dinner, had a lecture, made a visit, and went to bed on mattresses no thicker than your thumb and stuffed with comfy horsehair.

Although everything I have said in the last four paragraphs has been merely a matter of historical interest, and the practices therein described have faded unlamented from novitiate entrance days, I am sure the feeling of that first night was no different for a Jesuit in 1540 and will be no different for a

Jesuit in 2040. I lay there looking up at the cracks in the ceiling and groaned: "Oh . . . my . . . God! What have I gotten myself into!"

What I had gotten myself into was, of course, the Society of Jesus, and with unaccustomed wisdom I made a vow to myself that night as I stared helplessly at the ceiling, "I'll give it a year--to the hilt. I won't question my vocation till next July 30th. "

And since that night there has never again been a question in my mind about whether or not I should be a Jesuit.

... And How It Grew

Ignatius' experience with his own hectic spiritual and intellectual formation made him resolve that his men would not have to travel the same disjointed road he had stumbled along at the beginning, "wasting" half his life in trial-and-error, turning back, doing too much, ruining his body, spreading himself all over the map. His men would begin with the spiritual life and then, once their studies began, nurture that spiritual life by daily meditation and Mass, by open manifestation of their inner lives to the superior, by a yearly retreat, by spiritual reading, and by the very content of the course of studies itself.

The studies are sequential: first, arts and sciences which would raise the questions about man and his moral and physical universe. That opens into the study of philosophy. Then after philosophy, a chance to teach, to come from the world of ivory towers into the world of men, and to mold the abstract answers into words even boys can understand. Then into theology, to push the questions of philosophy into the realms of God and to see the answers enriched by examining them again in the light of the scriptures and the Fathers of of the Church. Then, once the man is ordained, he returns to

the novitiate as a working priest to pull together the whole
period of training in the second long retreat.

The Novitiate

Every man entering the Society of Jesus spends at least two
years as a novice. Initially, the task is to slow the man down,
to let the rat-race mentality ease out of him so that he can
see the world, as it were, from a distance, objectively, at
peace.

The adjustment is not unlike the one a man makes when he
gets married; or perhaps better, it is like being born again
into a new family with all the experience and habits of one's
previous eighteen years or so. And one does it without the support and "predictability" of the family he took for granted for
so long. He is dependent now on the Society for food, for money, for shelter, for his way of defining himself. It is a new
life.

It would be false to say that the adjustment is easy. Seeing
one's world and oneself as they really are can never be easy.
But the man who balks at that will find no life as a Jesuit.

Unlike the lurid accounts of "the power and secret of the
Jesuits," the methods of indoctrination are not those of the
Siberian camp. The first way a man is shaped into a Jesuit
is merely by living in a community of Jesuits, abrading against
one another, misjudging one another, learning to live together,
learning to be good friends with men you have not chosen but
who have been chosen for you by Somebody Else.

Secondly, you learn to pray, to set yourself against the
norm of the first Christian. Many begin to feel that the goal
is too far away. It's then that they have to be reminded that
even a minor-league Christian can learn from a pro. But
prayer takes silence, solitude, concentration, experimentation,
and above all, trust--qualities not frequently nurtured or even
respected in the world today. It takes a quiet courage that most
young men aren't aware they have.

A third method is the study of the Constitutions of the Society, the three hundred pages in which St. Ignatius detailed what he expected of the Society. It is a closely-written, complex document which needs patient probing and long hours of pondering.

Still another facet of the early training is the "experiments" each novice undertakes. St. Ignatius knew the ideals of his young men were not going to be shielded from contamination by protective cloister walls. A well-delineated daily order would not save his men from decisions of their own. They were going to be men on the move, men in the marketplace, men completely involved with the world and therefore prey at every moment to the world's ideals: beating out the other guy, taking care of old number one, settling for comfort rather than challenge. Moreover, Ignatius knew that it is easier to build castles in the air than to build their foundations on rock with bloody hands. As C. S. Lewis said, "It is easier to pray for a boor than to go and visit him." Tolstoy, too, pictured Russian nobles at the opera weeping at the torment of the heroine while their carriage drivers froze outside in the icy Moscow night.

Therefore while novices are in the first stage of forming their spiritual ideals, Ignatius wanted those ideals tested out in the open, pondered again, tested again, shaped, toughened, and proved for a lifetime of work. He wanted neither Don Quixotes nor Sancho Panzas, but a combination of the two.

And so in his second year novitiate the novice goes out for a month or so several times and works in a cancer hospital as an orderly, touches with his hands the suffering it is so easy to theorize about. Then he comes back to the quiet of the novitiate and with the director of novices has the time to make the experience a part of his inner life. Then he might spend another month teaching in a Jesuit high school or working in a soup kitchen or coaching retarded children; then back to the novitiate to mold the real and the ideal into a foundation for his apostolic life.

Years ago when most of the young men entering the Society were sons of wealthy families, these "experiments" were thought of as "humbling" tasks. Even washing the dishes or peeling potatoes was a test of conviction for a man who had had his bath drawn and his horses curried. For the young Americans used to, but not enthusiastic about, taking out the garbage, these tasks are not really humbling but rather intimidating. As a Jesuit one might be tempted to think of himself as sophisticated, concerned with art and ideas and politics. To such a man, emptying a bedpan can be a very salutary experience.

But the greatest way in which the Jesuit finds himself before the world and before God is in the month-long Spiritual Exercises. Enough has already been said about its content and sequence. It is the experience Jesus faced in the desert and Ignatius faced at Manresa. Step by step the novice is led through the Exercises, and yet the retreat director is only a guide, making suggestions, pushing a bit, holding back, trying most of all to keep out of the way. The real work is not his; the real work is the forging of a soul which can be done only by the novice himself and the Spirit of God.

The catalyst of these two years is, of course, the director of novices. He must be a knowledgeable man, but more than anything else he must be a wise man with courage enough to push when he must, with prudence enough to know when not to meddle. It is not a job for either the flighty or the fainthearted. In a word, the director must be preeminently sane.

My director of novices was Bill Gleason. He was a tough man who smiled rarely and who had a tabled vein in his forehead which acted much like a novitiate barometer. When it started reacting ever so slightly, we faded into the woodwork, fast.

He knew the Constitutions as well as most of us knew the Our Father. He knew that to hold onto the unworldly aspirations of Christ, men had to be tough, as tough as the world they took the message to. At that point in my life he was just the man I needed.

For two years Bill Gleason was the most important person in my life--feared, worshiped, trusted, hated, loved. His praise for a novice was as rare as his smile, so when you got either, you walked on air for a week. When he bawled you out, not just criticized you but really let you have it, you wanted to commit hara-kiri on yourself or mayhem on him. The two or three times he did it in my first year, I went into a john stall, locked the door, and bawled. When he did it in my second year, I'd kneel in the chapel and tell Jesus in no uncertain terms what he could do with William J. Gleason, S.J. Without my realizing, Bill Gleason was doing a very important thing to me: he was giving me guts.

At least for me, the word for Bill was "severe," not harsh, but severe in the sense that the lines of a building or a ship or a rock are severe: clean, unvarnished, trim. He was a man with no bric-a-brac mementos on his desk. He wanted everything reduced to its essentials. He wanted his poverty, his chastity, his obedience, his work, and his novices to be uncluttered, unromantic, unsullied. And he struggled might and main to chip away at his imperfections--and ours. We all heard rumors of his hairshirt. They could have been the kind of fables that surround a figure as central as he was to us. It is undeniable, though, that he chopped trees in the winter with no gloves, that his clothes were army surplus, and that the fourteen years he had been director were penance enough in themselves. It is no surprise then, that for him the ultimate Jesuit was the foreign missioner.

The missionary cannot help but live a life of poverty, and poverty is, at least analogously, the key to the Exercises and to Ignatius. Being poor is no great blessing; if it were, we would not have a war on poverty and Jesuits all over the world would not be working to eliminate it. The poverty of Ignatius is rather a simplification. Without a clutter of the world's goods to amplify and defend, a man is free for the people who need him. It's what Ignatius called detachment. And the missioner is, by his situation, automatically poor and detached. On the other hand, the professor in his study, the scholastic in his high school classroom, the pastor with an inner city school, even the man assigned to beg funds for the missionary, have to make compromises with the world. It is an age-old paradox that the message of the poor Christ cannot be preached today without money. When the world preaches the message of self-centeredness so efficiently, the Church must itself become efficient or be drowned by voices less lofty but more powerful. But efficiency takes money, and money brings attachments. Nonetheless, Bill Gleason always wanted us to emulate the simplicity of the missionary, no matter what our later work. He wanted us to check periodically to see whether our compromises had ceased to be adaptations and become surrenders.

For each work Jesuits are engaged in, there are Jesuit heroes to match: Ignatius for administrators, Bellarmine for theologians, Dan Lord for youth ministry. But to Bill Gleason the model for the Jesuit-as-Jesuit was Francis Xavier, the man on the move, untrammeled by wealth or family or preconceptions, searching out seed beds for Christianity where other men had not dared to go.

In the years since I was a novice I have found that there are other ways, other styles of bringing men to a living realization of Jesuit life. Perhaps they are better ways. Bill Gleason, at least then, might have considered them too complex, too soft. There were elements in his doctrine and in his methods that I know I would not approve of for novices today. But my idea of a Jesuit will always be strongly colored by what Bill Gleason believed and by who Bill Gleason was. He was one of the greatest men in my life.

One's novice director is important, but one's classmates are equally important. They are "the men in my year." A young man in the early years of the course is too involved with the concerns of the moment to realize that most of the men around him are the men with whom he will spend the next ten or fifteen years of his life, moving with them as a group from year to year, from stage to stage. Men in the army get to know their buddies very well and the camaraderie and shared pain can be an enriching experience. But this companionship lasts only a year or two and is gone. The companionship in the Society is for at least a decade. And it is in the Company of Jesus, in the fullest sense of the Latin roots of that word, cum-pane, men who break the Bread together. I suspect this is why many men, even when they leave the Society, still feel a part of "their year."

You can get to know a lot about a man in ten years when you are thrown together in different mixtures, chopping trees, playing ball, waxing floors, reviewing for exams. During our course of studies everything was shared, everything was "ours"; in fact, even we were Ours. The common life as Jesuits and the infinite facets of each one put a different tinge on all of us.

One of the men to whom I owe more than I've ever told him is Vinnie Butler. To a man who had checked in his cleats in second grade, the interminable round of seminary softball games was slightly more distasteful than a room full of bed-pans. One day, though, Vinnie Butler--who like myself was always shunted out of harm's way to someplace "safe" like second base or right field--got up to the plate, grabbed the bat, and said, "Which end of this thing do you hold?" Every-body laughed. Everybody understood. And nobody cared. By being himself Vinnie had made me freer to be myself.

Men like Joe Saunders and Jim Shea were built like marines, the one like a whippet, the other like a bear. They were among the super-jocks. But along with so many others they showed easily and unaffectedly that they cared about each other. It is a lesson too few men in America learn any more: that two men can honestly love one another without pretending they don't, that the commandment to love your neighbor need not be watered down to a pale concern nor restricted to the distaff side of the human race. It was one of the best lessons of my life.

Of all the men in my year, Ed Nagle has done most for me. He was the first man I was ever unafraid to cry in front of, and yet he was also the man who never lacked the courage and the love to tell me when I was making a damn fool of myself. I have more brothers than a man deserves who are friends as good as that, but Ed was the first. And the best.

Other men gave of themselves to me without realizing it.
Chief among them were the brothers in the kitchen and the old
men in the infirmary.

Joe Wuss and Peter Czalka were lay brothers who served up
the most delicious meals I've ever had in the Society. They
served 250 men, three times a day, seven days a week. You
can pay men to be as inventive or as hard-working as they,
but you can't pay men to be so unswervingly patient. One in-
cident will serve as an example.

One boiling summer day I was mopping the kitchen one level
below the refectory during lunch. Joe Wuss was putting away
the pots. Upstairs a novice was fiddling with the admittedly
tricky hand brake on the elevator. As happened so often, he
goofed. Suddenly with an apocalyptic crash the elevator came
down, dishes, leftover food, carts, and two open milk cans,
one with milk, the other with lemonade. Before I could even
gasp, the milk and lemonade were combining into great white
gobs.

Without the corners of his mouth moving one micro-milli-
meter, Joe Wuss stepped into the mess and started picking out
shards of dishware, and with only the trace of a sigh he said
to me, "Better start mopping this up, Brother." I don't know
how well I've made that lesson in patience part of myself, but
I can never say Joe Wuss didn't teach it to me.

Though no one admitted it and everyone acted otherwise,
the old men in the infirmary were there to die. In the province
catalog their apostolate was listed as "praying for the Society."
But old Brother McHugh would have none of that. He was deaf
as a doorknob and whispered in a voice that would fill Yankee
Stadium, and all day long while he "prayed for the Society"
he darned socks. That is, he would pull out the cloth around
the hole, stick a needle and thread through, and tie the thread
around the bulge into a nice fat rosette. When we pulled the
socks out of the common stock drawer, we could chose between
blisters or ripping the socks open again and wearing them with
the hole. It might have been useless work, but Mike McHugh

never knew it. He had worked all his life and he wasn't going
to quit then.

Since that time I've met other Jesuits who refused to give
up, men like Father F. P. Donnelly and Father Jim Mulligan.
"Skippy" McCaffrey who was a teetotaler and drank only "non-
alcoholic Benedictine, had been master of novices in English
Canada and master of novices in the Philippines and at eighty-
some years was blind and in the infirmary. Each night a scholastic volunteered to sleep in the next room with the door open
in case Father woke up and needed anything. He woke up, all
right. One night that I spent next door I leaped over the end
of my bed and into his room no fewer than twenty-eight times
because he was up and poking around looking for his socks
--two sleeping pills notwithstanding.

Being blind "Skippy" could only feel the dial on his braille
watch; and if he woke up and felt the hands at twelve or two,
he was terrified that it was afternoon and he had missed
saying Mass. That old blind man taught me to see better what
Mass means to a Jesuit.

There are so many others who made me grow--Paul, Bert,
Sal, Babe--and so little space for them here. But the purpose
of these pages is not to give gratitude to each of the people
I love but to indicate how Jesuits help one another to grow.
Let it be said that in the summer of 1953 when I went up the
altar steps and spoke my vows in front of the Host, there was
no question in my mind that these were men worth risking my
life on.

Juniorate-Philosophate

"Let them be shrewd as serpents and simple as doves. "

Ignatius' vocation grew in a time when very few priests
knew how to preach. Quite a few of them couldn't even understand the Latin prayers of the Mass. It was his goal that
Jesuits would be men with a firm personal grasp of the faith

who could also shape the language they used to the faith they professed. They were to be men who knew words and argument and rhetoric. The aim of the first part of the Jesuit course-- and in fact of all Jesuit schools--is a man possessed of <u>eloquentia perfecta</u>: articulate wisdom.

That's a nice compact formula, but like "rational animal" it is an impaction of complex skills and realizations. To be wise is one thing--it means experience-reflected-upon. Where wisdom is concerned, there are as many wise women who wring mops for a living as there are wise priests. Wisdom comes from living life, one's own life and the lives of others who have graciously bade us share their lives through their conversations and writing. But wisdom also takes reflection, a seasoning, an ingestion of experience into the whole fabric of one's life. The Curé of Ars can enrich me by the wise warmth of his companionable belief. Samuel Beckett can expand me by the wise chill of his lonely unbelief. But I must have time and the lonely hours of wrestling in order to make another man's experience my own.

Articulateness is another matter entirely. The wise mop-wringer can be tongue-tied by her lack of words and shackled to the redolent phrases and clichés by which old people pass wisdom from generation to generation. Conversely the empty debater can wring tears from judges for a proposition he neither believes in nor cares about. Words are a tool and they can be used either to expand or to exploit. No one in the history of man has used words and structures and pictures and music more corruptively than the amoral sirens of Madison Avenue. If the Church is to be heard, its wisdom must be as articulate as its opponent's.

What Ignatius wanted was a man who had met Jesus Christ in the Exercises. But he also wanted a man who had faced life in the world with utter honesty and with his critical faculties honed to discriminate between the holy and the hollow. And he wanted a man who could forge the truths of human life and divine life into a structure of words that would be clear and gripping whether his audience were Indians around a campfire or scholars at a convention or bishops at an ecumenical council--or all of them together at one time. What he asked for was the impossible combination one finds in every page of the gospel, the mysteries of man's divinization couched in the words of fishermen.

Any novelist worth reprinting and any philosopher worth a doctoral dissertation has wrestled with the basic questions of man: why was I born? why do I suffer? what will fulfill me? And Ignatius asks his men to listen to the answers that men have given to those questions, Chaucer and Dostoevsky, Spinoza and Aquinas, Sartre and Lonergan, and thereby enrich the gift they will bring when they bring themselves to God's people.

In brief, a Jesuit should be so prepared by his prayer and his studies that he is unafraid to speak to any man--be he a skid-row bum or a pope of Rome--of why man is alive.

In the Constitutions Ignatius writes, "They cannot do anything more pleasing to God our Lord than to study (for the glory of God and the good of souls). . . . Even if they never have an occasion to employ the matter studied, their very labor in studying, taken up as it ought to be because of charity and obedience, is itself work highly meritorious in the eyes of the Divine and Supreme Majesty."

And so the Jesuit, no matter what his future work, takes up English literature, Latin and Greek, chemistry, physics, math, modern languages, statistics, psychology and sociology, ethics, anthropology, economics, music, etc., etc., and a horrendous dollop of metaphysics. He takes far more than his contemporaries at an ordinary college, not because he will teach those subjects but so that he can have a quick survey of the fields he might serve and know what men do in fields other than the one he chooses for himself.

It is the ideal of the Renaissance Man; it is rarely realized in an individual Jesuit. But even our "almosts" are men we can justly be proud of.

Sounds terrific, huh? That was the quixotic dream that led me to the juniorate and philosophate. And it didn't materialize. At least not as I expected.

A bit of analogy. For awhile we had a young lay teacher at McQuaid High School in Rochester, New York who came there with the idea that Jesuits were a cross between Aristotle and Rabelais. Alas, before a month had passed, he was crestfallen. He had expected the teachers' fifteen-minute coffee break to be alive with chit-chat of Proust and Pavlov and Peanuts. On the contrary, the staple of conversation was last Saturday's football scores and the intransigence of the principal and the kid who squirted a stink bomb into the freshman lockers.

He had found that Jesuits were not gods but men. I went to the juniorate and philosophate with the same naive hope and found the same disconcerting reality.

What I write here about the juniorate and philosophate will be solely for historical completeness since the young Jesuit today takes all his formal courses not in sylvan seminaries but on urban college campuses. The course matter, though perhaps less intense, is still the same. And there were several men I met in these years who influenced my Jesuit life. Moreover, long years of study, no matter when or where, will always raise similar battles in a man's soul.

During my two years of novitiate we were only allowed to read ascetical books. After such a long hiatus the novel-junkie dove into the juniors' library with a near-demonic joy. Among other indulgences I read all the plays of Shakespeare and all the novels of Graham Greene and all the dialogues of Plato and all the works of innumerable other authors. And Ed Cuffe, that enchanted literary cicerone, started us off with druids gibbering around the portals of Stonehenge and led us through the whole of English lit up to the time of Elizabeth.

That year was a head-trip like a journey from Salem, Massachusetts into Shakespeare's London. We staged two plays that year for the whole community, Gogol's "The Inspector General" at Christmas and Sophocles' "Philoctetes" in February; and by the time we were finished I was ready for the chuckle farm. Unlike the novitiate there was no master in the juniorate except one's own prudence. And "by making mistakes, I learned not to make mistakes." For awhile.

Besides the two annual plays that each took a full month of preparation, we also had a Shakespeare Academy. (The Shakespeare Academy, methinks, is a lamentable loss in the new urbanization of the course.) Two of the profs would form a new group every couple of weeks to put on a longish scene from something like "Midsummer Night's Dream" or "Hamlet." Though they were anything but polished, the scenes had the great benefit of getting everybody onstage sooner or later, the timid and the blustery. For men who would occupy their lives teaching, preaching, and celebrating the liturgy, it was an invaluable experience. For men with no newspapers or TV or movies, it was a godsend. One performance, an evening of crowd scenes, will live in the lore of our year as long as Jesuits drink beer.

With the possible exception of a football field, there is no way to get to know men better than by sharing a stage with them for two weeks!

When I moved on from the juniorate to the philosophate, I had some of the best teachers I ever had. And some of the worst.

Joe Slattery was a volcanic treasure-house. As he said himself, "I have made my mind a sewer of print." And all that he had read was woven into lectures that were stupefyingly intricate leading off in all directions, literary, philosophical, scriptural, sociological, Ignatian, and yet knotted together at the core by one molten idea.

Joe was the kind of teacher who could say, "This book is absolutely the best example of such-and-such"; and as soon as the lecture was over, there'd be a logjam of scholastics at the library door to get the book first. Joe was salty, unpredictable, brilliant, maudlin, learned, crusty. A paragraph or two is too small for him; he deserves an epic poem. He was, in brief, the most stimulating teacher I ever knew.

In high school the only subject that ever threatened to scuttle me was physics, and I vowed on my life that only an encounter with the burning bush would drive me into a physics class again. It will come as no surprise then that every scholastic was required to take a year and a half of atomic physics in the philosophate.

Now I didn't give two hoots for Heisenberg, and I sat there grimly daring the physics prof to make me care. Tom Cullen was the man to do it. He knew the only reason his audience had been corralled was holy obedience and that most of us would prefer a season in hell to being in his class. So he turned out to be just about the most inventive pedagogue I ever encountered.

To show how electrons worked, he'd whirl his hands, his feet, his eyes, his head, and anything else within reach of his mind. He described the slightly untoward relationships between atomic particles in terms and tones more suggestive than a skin flick. We found that he practiced his class aloud every night before he actually gave it. He refused to insult even a hostile audience.

I still don't give many hoots for Heisenberg, but Tom Cullen opened my mind to a world I had locked out. What's more important, he taught me more about teaching than all the education courses I have ever endured.

Paradoxically my other greatest mentors along the line were the really poor teachers I have had. We had men who mistakenly presumed eager audiences, who dodged questions with smoke screens and fiddle-faddle and even ad hominems. We had men who tried to unscrew the inscrutable and left all the parts lying around in mind-boggling confusion. Some gave tests requiring an expanse of knowledge and memory of detail that no computer could accommodate.

But all of them without exception enriched me as a teacher. Over and over I vowed that if I survived I would never do those things to a class. And that is not an inconsiderable education.

The enemies of metaphysics mock it by saying that its prac-
titioners spend their lives trying to determine how many angels
can frolic on the head of a pin. We never tackled that one, but
at times I was almost groaning for something as concrete as
a pinhead. I had come to find the answers to the burning questions of man's existence and ended nearly drowning in the fog
of whether the essence of a thing is really distinct from its
existence or only notionally distinct. And we took such questions as seriously as Holy Writ and shunned such men as our
own Suarez as little better than a perverter of youth.

What had all this to do with the people who needed priests?
I chafed at its airy irrelevance, its serpentine circuits, down,
around, and through molehills, its ultimate vacuity. It was
splitting unreal hairs with an unreal pole axe. I had only one
life to live and in dull obedience I was squandering three
precious years of it on asininity.

In brief, I detested it.

And I wouldn't have missed it for the world.

Some people's vocations are tested and refined and given
substance by struggles with celibacy or with obedience or with
poverty. The inner wrestling sometimes goes on for years,
but the perseverance, the minor triumphs, and the ultimate
endurance leave the man stronger, richer, more fully in possession of himself. My crucible was metaphysics.

I am by nature a doer. "Don't bother me with theories; the
world's falling down around our ears!" If I hadn't been a priest-
teacher, I would probably have been a social worker or a poli-
tician or a soup kitchen executive, hopping on my horse every
morning and dashing off in all directions at once. So for me
the seven years of philosophical and theological abstractions
were a torture. And a godsend.

First it taught me obedience. There's no way I would have
stayed with _ens_ _ut_ _sic_ if it had not been for a Jesuit a _sine_
qua non.

Second it taught me patience. All the lessons Bill Gleason
had force-fed me began to pay off. And although several profs
thought I spent most of the day shooting the breeze, I was actu-

ally spending about eight hours a day digesting the theses to three pages, then to one page, then to a half-page, then to a three-by-five card. For seven years it was a debilitating grind. But Jacob toiled twice as long for Rachel.

Metaphysics also gave me the gift of concentration, what is known by less lofty terms to my peers as my brass butt. I can now work in a room with only books and paper for hours at a time without a break or a radio or cushy surroundings. Essential for a teacher.

Besides the discipline of perseverance, my stay in the philosophate taught me the discipline of logical order, the relationships between ideas, the use of progressively developing structure. Essential for a writer.

Finally it was a lesson in humility. I suddenly came up against two unavoidable realizations: one, there were more than a few men in my year who were far smarter than I was; and two, that there was a subject which people in charge considered essential for a good priest, and those same people considered my work in that subject at best mediocre. I had the marks to prove it.

This three-year slide into self-distaste increased till the end of my time in philosophy when it was capped by a judgment which I considered unjust. The judgment on my intelligence was made by the faculty. In my mind they had to be right. And the superior, the voice of God for me, concurred. In my soul he had to be right. The problem was that I also thought they were all dead wrong. This dilemma and its pain were not to be resolved till much later in theology, so I will leave the subject here and return to it later on.

These last paragraphs have not been pleasant to write, and I was strongly tempted to omit them since hardly any of the specifics are likely to recur in the lives of present-day scholastics. But that would be to adopt the sunny deception of so much vocation literature--which I promised to avoid from the outset. Although the specifics are different today, no man can avoid misunderstanding and an occasional even protracted sense of failure. If a man wants to be a Jesuit, it would be a cruel kindness to let him enter believing he could avoid the personal torments with which every man must wrestle for his manhood.

Regency

No cavalry brigade ever came more opportunely to rescue the beleagured fort than regency came to rescue me! If I had chafed at abstractions, itched to be active, craved some ac-knowledgment of my value to the Society, regency was tailor-made. Whoever invented it was a genius.

Just as the experiments of the novitiate were planned to keep the Jesuit constantly cross-feeding the ideal and the real, the active regency period comes in the middle of the course as a two- or three-year experiment in tempering idealism with real-ity. It involves teaching or working in the missions or helping in retreat houses or community organizing. At the very least, the Jesuit finds that the vast majority of the human race is not even slightly interested in the M. A. thesis he spent six months on.

Furthermore after living in a large structured community for six or seven years, the scholastic moves into a smaller group of men with less supervision and fewer visible supports. It is his first prolonged trial run outside the nest. He doesn't just pop in and out for a month but becomes an integral part of the community effort and is expected to pull his weight just like the long-time members.

Moreover this is not a group of starry-eyed young men. They are seasoned veterans, many of them edifying men who after years of work are still learning, still growing. Some, however, have settled into a routine and content themselves with doing the job. Some have become embittered. Some have given up. Regency is a crucible in which the scholar is tested and tempered into an apostle.

I don't know how many Jesuits considered Vinnie Watson a great principal. I do. He was not a great educator, but he surely was a great administrator. He was blessed with a layman who was a first-rate registrar and who kept the school running. This left Vinnie free to make the faculty reach toward better teaching. He didn't propose any specific ways in which to improve--he probably couldn't have. He drank slightly too much and read slightly too little. He was not an idea man but a gadfly. And he used any means, some of them questionable, to fire the scholastics up to better teaching. He could take you aside one day and say, "Look, O'Malley, be _bigger_ than Culkin, _bigger_ than Kilfoyle!" Then a couple of days later after a couple of beers he could say, "You'll _never_ be a teacher. You get all your ideas out of the _TV Guide._" He ran us like a boys club basketball team.

And he played dirty. One time he asked me how the school magazine which he had founded was going to do in the state competition. Before I could answer he said, "You'll _never_ do as well as I did. I got the highest score any magazine _ever_ got!" (A lot of what Vinnie said was in italics.) Naturally I girded up all my powers and I beat him. Which is just what he wanted. But even after I'd done it, he refused to admit I had.

Vinnie made us reach farther than we'd intended to. That, I think, is what makes a great administrator.

But how were we going to find specific ways to improve: how to organize a class, how to test and grade fairly, what books to teach? God knows not from Vinnie. He was the _agent provocateur._ But he knew that he had the best damn bunch of scholastics in the province, which he never tired of telling us and which we never tired of hearing. So for specifics we went to one another. Bill McCurdy was my undesignated master teacher, sharing his test stencils, breaking me in to take over the magazine, telling me how to dodge the rector, and most important, being a good enough friend to tell me when my new-found freedom was leading me into making an ass of myself. There were others: Dan Kilfoyle with his conviction that kids needed challenge not childish novels, Neil Doherty with his holy kindness,

George Driscoll with his indefatigable work. And when these men went on to theology, it was my job to help pass on the tradition to the new men coming out.

Vocations were high then and the thirteen regents were a sub-community unto themselves. We shared everything from our meager dollar-fifty-a-week allowances to our struggles to stay awake at seven o'clock Mass. When one man's students ran a dance, we were all there to help or at least to jeer things on. When Jimmy McNamara's yearbook came in and we discovered that one of the kids in a swimming picture had no bathing suit on, we all set to with erasers.

In regency the scholastic meets laymen for the first time not as subjects for conversion but as fellow apostles. There were old timers like Doc Quinn who never had his teeth in, Bob Nebot and Jack Devlin who had taught Latin for so long and so well that their classes were textbooks of clarity, Ed Bartley who spread aliveness and joy and simple love in a way I have never seen the likes of before or since. There were coaches and maintenance men, administrators and secretaries. And we were part of them as equals. And when we spoke, they listened and respected us. It was like being reborn again.

And there was Charlie Winans.

I'm not going to attempt to capsulize a man who defies both prose and poetry. More than once I've sat down thinking I'd cop a thousand clams from The Reader's Digest for a sketch of Charlie as "The Most Unforgettable Character I've Ever Met." No way. But as a layman Charlie was one of the most formative influences on my life as a Jesuit. And he demands at least an inadequate attempt at summary.

Charlie was the first fully real-ized Christian I ever met. He lived every day in capital letters. He had the body of Orson Welles and the soul of Francis of Assisi. God had made the world and saw it was good, and we should not insult God by not enjoying it. Charlie could drink till three, but he'd be up for Mass at six. Like Gulliver among the Lilliputians, he found the rules and lesson plans and deadlines of this life no more than the inventions of tiny men with tiny minds, mere threads he could tolerate or snap as he chose. He taught classes and directed plays with broad strokes, expansive, bellowing, bellying, leaving details like memorizing lines to the fear and adrenalin of the last week, leaving details like getting an auditorium to the long-suffering Jim Breininger. He took kids to the opera, to plays, to films, to dinner in Manhattan, to Irish bars and Greek bars and Russian bars. He opened up a whole realm of learning about life and people to tough Brooklyn kids. He gave no thought to whether the kids could or would pay their share with the result that he was always writing checks for a hundred dollars and wondering why the bank was always stealing from his checking account.

Charlie was above turmoil. One example will have to suffice although there were hundreds in the three joyful years I was fortunate to share with him. We were doing "The Mikado": Charlie the dialogue, I the songs and dances. One of the Jesuits had put on the show at St. Peter's in Jersey City and told us about a combo he had hired that "set the kids on fire!" So Charlie and I hustled over to Jersey, saw the guy, and though he looked less pyrotechnic than advertised, we engaged him. Did he need orchestral scores? "Naw, jussa coupla p'yanna score. Dey knew da 'Muck-oddo' so well dey could do it in'air sleep. "

The combo wasn't due to show up till the dress rehearsal; but a week before, the man called to say "he couldn't get no p'yanna playah. " We searched and searched and finally came up with the manager of the local chain grocery who reputedly had played with the Vienna Symphony. It was hard to tell since his English wasn't so hot and he'd never heard of the "Muckoddo. " A day before the dress rehearsal the band man called that "he couldn't get no drummah. " We got a father of one of the kids who'd played traps in college twenty years before.

The night arrived--costumes, make-up, lights! And the combo. Surely, there was never a more mismatched gaggle of bald-pated and acned music makers ever assembled. Undaunted, I climbed down into the pit, took up the baton and said, "Okay. Let's try the overture. Ready? One-two-three-four, one-two-three-four. " I gave the downbeat.

Nothing.

"Maybe we all don't have the right place. It's page one?
Okay. Ready?"

There followed the most cacophonous disjuncture of wheezes,
squeals, rasps, and rat-a-tats ever visited upon the ears of
man.

"Okay, then. Let's skip the overture for awhile, shall we?
Let's start at the first number. You guys ready in the wings?
Okay. Now!"

It was godawful. I'm sure there's a place in heaven for high
school drama directors right next door to martyrs who have
been hanged, drawn, and quartered. The Gentlemen of Japan
came mincing along the lip of the stage and peered into the
pit as if it were populated by a tangle of inimical gryphons,
camelopards, and godzillas.

At the end of the first horrific act I sat trembling with
Charlie in the back of the auditorium.

"Charlie, what in God's name are we gonna do?"

He stretched amiably, smiled and said, "No problem. Simply pay them and send them on their way. "

It was that simple. Money was only money, but the show was
the show. We got the two rehearsal pianists out of class all the
next day to practice till their fingers were blistered. And we
were boffo.

Charlie also gave me the best lesson I've ever had as a
teacher: he treated kids as adults, or practically adults. After
all, as Dan Lord said, that's what they are.

Charlie Winans taught me how to direct, how to teach, how
to cure a hangover, how to rise above the slings and arrows of
outrageous fortune, but most of all how to be a Christian. It's
odd that I had been a Catholic for twenty-six years and a religious for seven years before this great man showed me what
the gospels were really about: to give and not to count the cost,
to struggle onward and damn the small minds, to be used until
you're used up--even by people unworthy of your gift.

Above all though, even above Charlie, regency for me
meant the kids.

The boy in Brooklyn in 1957 and the boy in Rochester in 1977 are not that different. Under the patina of whatever the current sophistication is, they were and are gangly in body and soul, groping for an idea of who they are and what life is about, slavishly aping the studs, shy, brash, generous, self-centered, good. Father Flanagan of Boys Town said there's no such thing as a bad boy, and twelve years with them has shown me no evidence to the contrary. I've seen hurt boys and dumb boys, boys whose pent-up frustrated need to be loved flashed out in cruelty and thoughtlessness and destruction. I've seen more than a few good boys who did bad things. But I've never met a bad boy.

And when you are willing to show them unabashedly that you love them, by lambasting their foolishness, praising their modest progress, consoling their modest failures, showing your trust by challenging them, pinching their butts, then the hundredfold you receive in return is beyond a man's power to describe or even to fully comprehend.

After three years of feeling valued without any need to question it, I went back to four more years of metaphysics.

Theology

Well not quite metaphysics, at least not the fog-wrestling of philosophy.

After a few courses in biblical Greek and a few in the methods of theological investigation, a Jesuit's theology studies are divided into six major areas: scripture, dogma, church history, canon law, pastoral studies, and a few how-to-do-it courses in the rubrics of the Mass and the sacraments.

Scripture is the bedrock, the faith-experience out of which the Church emerged. The theology student, therefore, spends a great deal of time exploring the history, language, and thought-patterns of the Hebrew people and the early Church to discover how those people expressed their experience of God's revelation to them. Dogmatic theology studies the pronouncements of the

Church, the words and formulas it has used to express its deepening understanding of the scriptures over its two-thousand year history. Moral theology and canon law reflect the Church's attempt to formulate codes of conduct by which the Catholic can make choices of action. Pastoral studies try to find concrete ways in which the life of the gospels can be preached and celebrated meaningfully.

As in philosophy the entire year's work is summarized into theses which each student has to defend orally before three examiners, a half-hour for moral and canon law, another half-hour for dogma and scripture. There are about thirty theses for each exam, and the student has to be able to explain each thesis, substantiate its claims in scripture, in the Fathers of the Church, the ecumenical councils, and in the practice of the Church. He has to defend the thesis and any of its ramifications against the arguments of adversaries over the last two thousand years.

Let me tell you, it's a fun-packed half-hour. And in my time it was in Latin, as were the lectures, the class notes, and the textbooks. Mercifully they are all in English now.

At the end of his third year of theology the scholastic is ordained a priest, and while he continues his studies, he begins to work in parishes, hospitals, prisons, and orphanages.

A priest needn't know theology in order to say Mass. All that requires is an ability to read, a knowledge of the movements, and authorization by the Church. Theology does come in handy, however, when you preach or hear confessions or counsel, or teach Christian doctrine. The good priest should be kind of an expert in things theological although he needn't be a theological encyclopedia. After all, the Curé of Ars, the patron of parish priests, did quite well as a priest after flunking theology exams with astonishing regularity. Ignatius himself never came near being the top man in his class. Unfortunately, in the midst of the real thing, one tends to forget that.

When I first went to Woodstock, Maryland, the word "theologian" was a rarefied term applied only to the professional theologizer and the future seminary professor. As Gus Weigel told us the first day of class, "For some of you this will be a school of theology, for the rest it will be a barber college. " I bristled at his condescension, but as the years dragged on I wondered if I was even going to learn how to cut hair!

In my mind the greatest justification for moving seminaries to urban campuses is that the scholastics now mingle with other students of the same subjects. In the seminaries sequestered in the country the courses could be more high-powered simply because of a select group of highly motivated students undistracted by other activities and other responsibilities. About the only thing one could do was study theology. It was a highly efficient set-up.

The psychological drawbacks, however, were enormous. If you siphon off the cream of the crop and set it aside from the rest, there still must be a top, a middle, and a bottom to that extraordinary group of men. Anyone at the bottom of such a class could possibly be near the top of any larger homogeneous group. But he is actually at the bottom of his class, and being hundreds of miles from the nearest comparable group, the Jesuit was likely to get pretty down on himself. After all, flunking, with all its psychological ramifications, is still flunking.

The teaching in those restricted seminary classes was pitched to the cream of the cream of the crop. And that is a legitimate educational option since the best are not left unchallenged and the lower levels are driven to reach higher than they might have otherwise. But many men who have eventually made excellent priests felt for the first time the experience of real failure. Which is not a bad experience for any man. But when it continued for so long a time, many who objectively should have called themselves "toward the bottom of the best" instead called themselves "just stupid. "

What I have just described is in great part an educational and psychological situation which no longer exists. Seminaries of the future need never fear this specific gauntlet. However, I know of no man of the mind, no man of intrepid spirit, no

man who truly and integrally possesses himself who did not go
through a similar "dark night of the soul. " This was mine.

It is remarkable how stupidly I handled it.

The material of first year was rather good: the nature of the
Church and the scriptural and doctrinal study of the historical
Jesus. But for a man of previously simple faith, it did pose its
problems.

At the end of Joe Fitzmyer's first year scripture course, I
who had learned better than to raise my hand back in philosophy
raised my hand and asked, "Father, since we're not trying to
prove that the four evangelists wrote the gospels, have we
been trying to prove that no matter who wrote them the authors
at least knew what they were talking about?"

"No. "

Tailspin.

But it was a valuable tailspin. For more than a month the
only thing that kept me in the Church (much less in a celibate
seminary) was the fact that the two scripture professors who
knew far more about the troublesome problems of scripture
than I did still said Mass every morning. Their actions spoke
louder than my inability to fathom their words. Finally, much
later, after a searing and protracted crisis of faith, I realized that there is no proof for the existence of God or an after-
life or forgiveness or grace, no proof such that, once he understands the alternatives, a reasonable man could not have the
slightest doubt or hesitation. If there were, all the people outside the Church would be dumb.

For all the texts and theses and arguments the only answer
to my crisis was the answer of faith, a calculated risk that we
are not ridiculous ants crawling on this dull cinder in the cold
of space, but sons of the most high God. Being a Christian was
not a way of securing my life but rather a way of betting it. It
was an "answer" less assuring but infinitely more exciting,
and it came not from a textbook but from prayer and pain and
the patient willingness of my confessors and friends to explain
it all to me "just one more time. "

Perhaps the root cause of that first year's pain, and the second's, and the third's, was the loneliness. Or perhaps more precisely, the dependence I had had for so long on the approval of other people as the foundation of my self-image. For three years at Brooklyn Prep I had been treated by the kids and the faculty and the parents as a person, respected, esteemed, even loved. For three years there had not been even a shadow of a doubt that I was worthwhile to the people of God and to the Society of Jesus.

Now, though, I was one man in two hundred. Every morning I walked into the refectory and saw all those anonymous black backs bent over their oatmeal and wondered if I still had a name and a face and dreams anymore. The monochromatic life begins to play tricks on your eyes. All day I sat in class with sixty or a hundred bodies. All my free time I spent alone in a room nine by nine by nine feet with a desk, a bed, a shelf of books and (I hoped) the Holy Spirit. And he was fading fast.

What I didn't understand until far later was that my problem of faith was not really rooted in my doubts about God but in my doubts about myself. If I were the "bucket of scum" I felt myself to be, the loss of God would simply be the masochistic rejection of the last prop to any sense of personal value. I was one sorry mess, I was.

There were breaks, an occasional beer party, a picnic, a nice day. But to the man drowning in self-pity even sunshine looks bleak. It means that sooner or later it's going to rain and storm and flood and we'll all die and maybe that's best. God, it was awful. And it lasted over two years. And it was mostly my own fault.

I look back on it with both shame and pride, shame that I'd focused the value of the whole universe within the confines of my own skin, pride that I must have manifested at least the faintest vestige of value since my friends refused to desert me, even when my incessant hawking of my abysmal confusion must have made me an unbearable hemorrhoid.

As the years dragged on, classes became more and more tedious. It was all so arcane, so irrelevant, so divorced from the needs of the people I had known in regency. I didn't want to push back the theological frontiers; I just wanted to be a good, intelligent priest. But "they" kept requiring me to stuff my mind with data I could neither comprehend nor remember nor care about.

The combination of loneliness, futility, and self-pity is not pretty from the inside or, I fear, from the outside. But I continue to flog it to death here so that anyone so tempted may see its idiocy. It was a vicious circle: the more I failed to understand the theology, the more I turned inside my detestable self, the more I wallowed in self-distaste, the more distant and unfathomable the theology became. And on and on and on into the night.

There were palliatives aplenty had I opened my eyes.

Terry Toland who was the dean was also a prince. Once a year at Thanksgiving he shipped me off to the English Teachers' Convention, first in Chicago, then in Philadelphia, then (incredibly) in Miami Beach! His only stipulation was I should make some comment in whatever meetings I attended. It was balm to a sore mind. For those three days each year, I was given evidence, clearly, that I had something to say and was respected for saying it. But within a week I'd have forgotten it.

Every summer Neil Carr, my provincial, sent me to McQuaid High where I acted as a master-teacher for the new regents. I taught the McQuaid summer school students with the scholastics in the back of the class and gradually turned the whole class over to them. At the same time Paul Naumann and I were formulating a completely new four-year syllabus for the province's high schools. It was an exhilarating two months every year, but like every good pessimist I let it be haunted by the growing awareness that the days were dwindling down to a precious few and September meant I had to go back to prison.

But the best palliative of all: I put on shows--funny, crazy, zany, lovely shows. Like my "decision" to become a Jesuit, my "decision" to put on musicals was no more cerebral or studied than a drowning man's "decision" to gasp for air.

The arch lifeguard was Larry Madden. When Larry was in first year theology and I was in second, we staged a musical version of "Teahouse of the August Moon" which we had written in philosophy but never produced. It was--as so many other gifts in my life--another godsend. It cost us about a month of afternoons and about thirty dollars, but the dividends to all of us, cast and crew and combo and audience, were enormous. We got to know one another. We created something where before there had been nothing. We shared the show and ourselves.

The day after the show John Courtney Murray, an internationally known theologian, the subject of a cover story in _Time_, the seemingly aloof eminence of the whole theologate, stopped me in the corridor. I was overwhelmed that he even knew who I was! But with that courtly kindness which was his he said, "Bill, that play! The music, the lyrics, the acting--the _mise en scene_! They were sew-perb!" Gasp.

After that we did one original musical a year. There were some, even among my peers, who sniffed, "They're not here to put on shows. They're here to study theology!" But for a month each year I forgot I was reputedly dumb. I even forgot to be dumb. In a word, I forgot myself. I was closer to an answer than I realized.

Larry Madden--that calm, talented, chuckling, holy man-- had kept my head above water, not by solving my "problem" but by ignoring it. Let the lesson not be lost.

When I think back on it, the whole thing was really so stupid. I was the luckiest man in the world and too blind to see it. It's no wonder that last year a man from my class could say, "I always envied you through the course; you had it so easy, so much success, so much attention." And I did. The only one who didn't see it was me.

More than one faculty member, Tom Clark, Gus Weigel, Walter Burghardt, and others, gave of their time at least to "tide me over" till the next abysm. And if Jerry McMahon got a dollar an hour for all the time he manned the pumps of the sinking ship, he could pay off the national debt. But it was Ed

Nagle who wisely, instinctively, painfully gave me the only answer I really needed, the one all the others had been too kind
to give: "I'm sick and tired of listening to your damn self-
pity over and over and over. Now get the hell out of my room
and for God's sake stop it!"

It was like a hard slap in the face.

But it was the liberating blow one gives to a senseless hys-
teric. It was one of the kindest gifts I have ever been given.

So I went to the man I feared most, the man who could make
me leave the Society, or after eleven years of waiting postpone
my ordination which was now only a year away. The rector,
Ed Sponga.

Ed had been a tough kid from South Philly and ended up doing
a doctoral thesis in France on the philosophy of Maurice Blondel.
Like all the giants along my way, he was a complex man: iras-
cible and holy, moody and loving, kindly and tough. When he
later left the Society, I was truly shocked. But if Ed decided to
change his vocation, I could never have criticized his decision.
He was, after all, the man who saved mine.

When I had slowly dredged up the whole ugly thing once
again for him, he put down his head and sat there silently for
awhile. Then he gave his little grunt and said, "Engh. Why
don't you go see a shrink?"

The Moment at the Pump

For years and years Annie Sullivan drew signs in Helen Keller's
hands. It must have been a heroic frustration, day after day,
playing the game in the uncomprehending hands. There must
have been times when Annie had to hold herself back from
striking that brilliant dullard of a child and saying, "Understand, damn you! See!"

And finally it happened. Helen was out in the yard and her
shoulder happened to hit the handle of the pump. She felt vibra-
tions somewhere and she was curious. She hit the handle again

and reached out her hands. They were wet. Something inside her was beginning to connect; something choked up into her throat. And from her twisted mouth came the only word she could remember from her babyhood before the darkness: "Wah-wah."

It had happened. Helen Keller had discovered that things have names, that there were other persons beyond the darkness. She had made the most liberating discovery a human being can make, she had discovered that she was not alone. And she ran to Annie and in her hand she spelled "teacher."

My teachers were Dr. James Whedbee and, I have not the slightest doubt about it, the Holy Spirit of God.

Any hesitation I had about seeing a psychiatrist did not arise from the so-called "shame" one is supposed to feel if others discover you are cuckoo. The liberation of finally admitting that I needed more than just first aid from my confessors and friends was enough to smother that. Besides, there were enough other seminarians who also took the "psychmobile" to Baltimore twice a week, and they appeared sane enough to me, as sane as I must have appeared to them. I wasn't nuts, just sliding in that direction.

The hesitation came from the fact that I was putting my ordination on the block. My reading and my painfully sensitive antennae told me that one does not make a major change in his way of life, a change as radical as acceptance of the priesthood while he is still in the middle of therapy. But if I had contracted tuberculosis or hepatitis or some physical disease, there would have been no doubt or hesitation that it had to be taken care of, no matter what. So, however fearfully, I went.

Jim Whedbee. He was a quiet man, gentle, almost brooding, occasionally even jittery but in such a veiled way that it was months before I noticed it. When he listened he was completely passive on the outside, but inside he listened with all his ears. I often asked myself how a man could stand eight hours a day of listening to the twisted outpourings from the secret places of men and women, sharing them, trying ever so delicately and nondirectively to help them discover themselves by themselves. I remember thinking it must be like being nailed inside a confessional for life.

The infuriating part--and of course the key to the whole process--was that he never told me anything. Twice a week for months I sat there and talked. And talked. And talked. He'd nod, ask a question, nod, and I'd talk some more. Without knowing it I was using the educated man's smoke screen on him, cerebralizing. I knew chapter and verse what was wrong with me, causes and effects, Part I, A, 1, a, (1)--all intellectual structure, all head-trip, all pure balderdash. If I "knew" so well, why was I messed up? Why were the intellect and the realization so divorced from one another? The trouble was that I didn't know. The full self--not just the head but the heart and the imagination and the guts--didn't comprehend, appreciate, accept . . . love . . . who I was. Finally when I suddenly sat forward and said that to him, he smiled his soft smile and said, "Good. "

The sessions were interrupted by the regular salvific summer at McQuaid and began again in September when I returned to Woodstock. I saw very little progress, though I presume now that there must have been quite a bit. At the very least I was not inundating my friends with my problems. But then it began to be November. Then December. The time was narrowing down for me to make the decision: was I going to be ordained in June or not? Should I order invitations? Should I sign up the parish church for my first Mass? Should I tell my mother that the twelve-year wait was going to be longer?

I talked it over with the spiritual father of the house. About ten thousand times. And each time it was like talking to a recording:

"Should I be ordained or shouldn't I? I'm torn between thinking I definitely shouldn't and thinking I should. "

"What does the doctor say?"

"Well, in general, that people in therapy shouldn't make such life-changing decisions. "

"Then do what the doctor says. "

But that was too simple, too cut-and-dried, and it "felt" wrong, terribly wrong. I was heartened a bit when I told Dr. Whedbee what the spiritual father had said and he showed me a fury that I'd never seen before and never saw again: "Dammit! you've got to be able to talk to somebody in the line of faith, somebody who's not a scientist!"

At last it came. It was a Sunday morning in January. There was no time left. Just before lunch I'd gone to the spiritual father for another run around the track: "Should I . . . what does the doctor say . . . no changes . . . do what the doctor says. " When I left his room, all the others were going to lunch, but I went back to my room. I fussed and fretted and I paced. I knew I should be ordained, but how could I justify it? God! How long I paced, I don't know, but I did it until I just couldn't stand it any more. I had to get away from it. I'd go to bed. I lay down, but I didn't go to sleep. How long I lay there, I'll never know but it must have been a couple of hours. There were no thoughts I could remember, no logical arguments, just blindness.

Then suddenly it happened.

It was like a thunderbolt. It was like palpable grace. I sat up in bed, thunderstruck, and I said, "I'm a good man!"

It was like being reborn from the dead. Which is precisely what it was.

"I'm a good man! And I'll be a good priest because I'm a good man!"

It was the first time in thirty-two years that the pseudo-humble, pseudo-abnegated fool in me had let me see the truth! The God-ridden, shining, liberating truth!

I grabbed my ice skates and ran or tumbled or flew out of the house and I was all alone. And I skated around and around and around in huge circles and I shouted it aloud at the top of my voice, "I'm a good man! And I don't need anybody to tell me! I'll be a good priest because I'm a good man!"

It was my moment at the pump. It was the greatest grace I have ever had in my life, and since that moment--may God be praised--the liberation of it has never left me. Since then, even when I've been a fool, even when I have sinned, I knew it was a good man who did it.

The next day was Monday, and I had an appointment with Dr. Whedbee. I sat down and I said, "I have something to tell you. I'm going to be ordained no matter what you think of me. No matter what anybody thinks of me. I'll be a good priest because I'm a good man. No matter what anybody thinks. "

Slowly the smile spread across his face, and very, very quietly he said, "Good. "

On June 19, 1963 I climbed the steps of the chapel at Canisius College in Buffalo as a good man and I came down the steps as a good priest.

I spent another full year with Dr. Whedbee, delving into that marvelous moment, shoring it up, making it unbreakable. But the best moment in the two years was the first session when I came back to Woodstock after my ordination summer. When I finished the hour, I stood up to leave and Jim Whedbee, that good man, got down on his knees and said to me, "Father, could I have your blessing?"

It was a moment no man deserves.

Whatever I do as a priest, whatever I do as a Jesuit, I have to share--with my parents and Sister Mary Cecilia and Sister Mary Denis, with the Jesuits at Canisius and Holy Cross, with Bill Gleason and Joe Wuss and "Skippy" McCaffrey, and Ed Cuffe and Joe Slattery and Ralph Dates and John McMahon, with Vinnie Watson and Charlie Winans, with Larry Madden and Joe Fitzmyer and Jerry McMahon. I owe my life and my work as a priest to all my brothers, to those who left and those who stayed, to the world-beaters and the self-beaters, to the dynamic, the timid, the kindly, and the tough. They helped make me all I am, and who I am is a Jesuit priest.

But most of all, I owe it to Ed Nagle and Ed Sponga and Jim Whedbee. And to the undeniable Spirit of God.

Jesuits of the Future III

. . . arguably the most remarkable company of men to
embark on a spiritual journey since Jesus chose the
twelve Apostles . . . a bewilderingly diverse frater-
nity. They are seismologists, swamis, architects and
engineers, theologians and winemakers, politicians,
lawyers, social workers, revolutionaries, economists--
as well as missionaries, teachers and parish priests.

Time, 23 April 1973

And Time could have added psychiatrists and presidential ad-
visors, congressmen, and administrators, even a couple of
clowns, even a couple of ex-movie actors.
   The present-day Society of Jesus which a new novice will
enter embraces not only a diversity of occupations but a radical diversity of political and social and even theological views.
In our ranks we have both Christian Marxists and Christian
Birchers. We have Bob Drinan in the Congress, a Democrat,

and we had John McLaughlin as a presidential advisor, a Republican, who publicly demanded that Drinan resign. And besides these extremes, we have men at every notch of the spectrum between them.

To some men this embodies a confusion which is intolerable; men of such widely divergent views should seek their salvation elsewhere than in the Society of Jesus. Ignatius did not envision a Society of companionable pussycats. He wanted a band of tigers who would spread fire on the earth. And fire often burns even the men who light it. As Father Herbert de Souza has written, "There will always be a split among thinking men, especially devoted thinking men, in a crisis situation. They will often clash head-on because of a common devotion. " And as long as the clash is in the name of Jesus Christ and in the name of the Society we share as brothers, we will survive and thrive. Without that unifying Personage, though, and that bond of brotherhood beneath our differences, we are doomed.

We are called to live as colonists in the world, "on the ragged edge of nowhere. " And the only Jesuits I personally find difficult to embrace are the few who don their collars and their S.J. 's only on their way to a talk show or a riot.

But among the publicly noncontroversial Jesuits there is also a tension, especially about what Jesuits should be doing.

There are men who argue that we ought to be working with the influential--the kings, presidents, bishops, captains of industry--who have the power to change the face of the earth for the poor. And they are right.

There are men who argue that we ought to be working directly with the forgotten--the black, the chicano, the immigrant, the small businessman--who have the crying needs which no one else is willing to hear. And they are right.

There are men who argue that we ought to be working on the international level--the U.N. , UNESCO, the Organization of American States--for the victims of plague and over-population and ecological suicide. And they are right.

To me the antagonism between these positions seems to be a sterile struggle, an unconsciously self-aggrandizing posture which says equivalently, "You must do my work. Unless a Jesuit is (storming the barricades); (running a soup kitchen); (teaching retarded children); (giving retreats); (teaching in high school); (all of these); (other); he is not a true Jesuit."

At least at the moment we have enough Jesuits to serve in all these areas--and more. The problem lies rather in who has the priority, who gets the few men who are available, and in what proportions. Part of the solution, I believe, is in the hands of the Spirit who sends us men and who motivates our individual choices of ministry. The remainder of the solution is in the hands of superiors who must discern the minds of the Jesuits and the mind of the Savior we serve, and then make a decision.

But I agree with the restless who see that our numbers are dwindling while needs are expanding and the time for a statement of priorities is imminent. The American provincials are even now in the midst of gathering data for just such a decision in an effort called "Project I." This is the Society that a man of the 70's and perhaps even the 80's will join, a Society in transition. It will not be a settled monastic routine where one needs only to put himself into the hands of a four-hundred-year-old rule and an all-knowing superior. It will be into an organization which is by its nature and by the will of its founder always teetering on the frontier, trying still again to discern what are the absolute nonnegotiables in Jesuitness and then trying, imaginatively, to carry that intuition into new forms in a new world. Perhaps, too, we must pour new life into old forms which we see are dying but are worth the commitment of our lives to save.

As Socrates said, "The unexamined life is not worth living." To rethink the elements of Jesuit life that have always seemed nonnegotiable is a salutary effort for the young man thinking of entering the Order as well as for the long-time Jesuit seeking to refurbish his ideals. I have done that rethinking for myself and, for what it is worth, I share it here.

If there are no nonnegotiables, if there is nothing that all of us and each of us agree is the irreducible minimum for continuing membership, if the essential core of what a Jesuit means can change arbitrarily with the passing of years, then we have no fellowship with Ignatius Loyola. We are no more than a variety of selves joined only by the convenience of a common label and a partly communal subsidy.

The Nonnegotiables of Jesuitness

There are Jesuits presently lobbying within the Society for the immediate surrender of all our brick-and-mortar institutions on the grounds that we have already brought them to workable status and they could be turned over to laymen. Such holdings, they argue, are a violation of our communal poverty and, as such, limit our mobility and our freedom, the freedom not only to choose new works but to give honest witness against the immoral business policies of some of the very benefactors who keep the schools open. On the other hand, there are Jesuits who are lobbying for personal credit cards and unsupervised checking accounts. And this second group is not necessarily distinct from the first.

There are Jesuits lobbying for a more modern assessment of the vow of celibacy. There are Jesuits who advocate an open rejection of repressive strictures on masturbation, homosexuality, premarital sex, and so on. On the other hand there are Jesuits who are lobbying for a return to the "old time religion."

There are also Jesuits who argue for a freer relationship between the provincial and the individual religious. They say, at least as I understand it--and I admit to a prejudice here-- that the superior should trust in them and in their reading of the Spirit's movement in the Church and in their own lives. Then, as God does, the superior should ratify their choices even if the choices might turn out to be destructive. They will bear the burden of their own mistakes. On the other hand, there are Jesuits who would like every man who steps out of line drummed unceremoniously out of the corps.

These are extremes, perhaps even caricatures, but they define the outer limits of two positions.

Poverty is, I think, negotiable as long as the man's honest inner urge and conviction is toward simplification rather than amplification of the worldly goods he has and uses. Ricci wore silk and De Nobili wore rags, both for the honor and glory of God. One Jesuit, at least with the later and tacit permission of his provincial, had a $450 a month apartment at the Watergate, while another Jesuit in ostensibly the same apostolate lived in the regular Jesuit community at Georgetown University. Both men had the same provincial. As a fellow Jesuit I am allowed an opinion, however ill-advised. But not being the provincial for either man, I am not allowed a decision.

Especially in the area of poverty, we have an infinite capacity to kid ourselves, coming to the conclusion that we really can't work effectively without a stereo or that our work is amplified by a new set of golf clubs. On the other hand, there are crypto-Puritans among us who insult their noncomprehending audiences by their tatters as much as Ricci would have insulted his mandarins by receiving them in patches.

It is the yearly retreat and the yearly manifestation of a man's conscience to his superior that saves us from negotiating the nonnegotiables.

To my mind chastity is negotiable only in the sense that the priest can break his vow and be forgiven—just as the first pope was forgiven his absolute denial of Christ though it was within hours of his ordination and first communion. Furthermore, a man's sexual preferences may be for women or other men or gorillas or corpses; but if he takes a vow, let him keep it. And just as I spare him public declarations of my foibles, I would prefer him to spare me his. If a man does not wish to be celibate, I wish him well in his expectation of a married clergy or in his marriage now, but at least to my mind actual celibacy is a nonnegotiable of Jesuit life. If it were otherwise, we might as well admit that the religious state is no more than a conglomerate of do-gooders.

The casual sexual liaison, even for a layman, demeans
sexual self-giving to little more than shaking hands or necking; and the protracted sexual liaison must by its very nature
lead to marriage or to heartbreak, or both. Proponents of
halfway measures or "third ways" are as childish as those who
want to be rich and poor at the same time. Fish or cut bait.

Obedience is negotiable all the way up to the last word. The
superior has that. A Jesuit can woo, blackmail, cajole, threaten,
banter, beg. Personally I believe that the faith of obedience
comes not in accepting uncritically the first "no" of a superior
but in "hammering on his door without ceasing," returning
again and again with new versions of the plan, new intimidations,
new inducements. But when the superior finally says, "That's
it, " that's it.

If it were otherwise, a man might as well live in a subsi-
dized bachelor hotel.

Ultimately, though, the one element that is ineradicably
the hallmark of a Jesuit is that he has in his most honest heart
the conviction that God is working through him in this organization of men.

The Society of Jesus is not a brotherhood of bonhomie and
benevolence like the Lions Club. Nor is it an educational union
like the NEA. Nor is it a coalition of convenience like a parliament without a plurality. It is not even a group of men who
believe in God and in Jesus Christ like the Church itself or
like another religious order.

It is a group of men, however chaotically disparate, who
have met Jesus Christ through Ignatius Loyola and who vow
themselves to service in the Church according to the Constitutions of the Society of Jesus.

Unlike a club or union or coalition, the Jesuit Order coheres
around a person, the transtemporal presence of the God-Man
Jesus Christ. The person of Christ is not merely a figurehead
like Abraham Lincoln, around whom men of only remotely
similar aspirations can still rally, nor a dearly revered
founder like John D. Rockefeller, whose name is the only rem-
nant of his effect on those gathered under it. Jesus Christ is the

reason for our being and the reason for our being together. It is to seek a deeper awareness of his alive presence that we "waste" valuable apostolic time in our prayer. It is the transcendence of his vision that allows us to see, with whatever pain, our momentary failures in the perspective of his eternity.

I confess that I shudder a little when I hear my Jesuit brothers preaching the gospel as if its sole core were the care of the neighbor--feeding the hungry, clothing the naked, visiting the imprisoned. This is a challenge we share with the atheist social worker, philanthropic foundations, the Shriners, and the Boy Scouts. There is nothing specifically Christian or Jesuit about such laudable effort unless it is done not only for my brothers but for my Brother. There are, after all, two commandments of the New Testament. Without the transcendent presence of Jesus Christ within our apostolic work, we are no more than good-hearted sociologists with crosses on our helmets.

The Society of Jesus is also unlike any other religious order. The men whose lives we have seen in this book are organically united not only by the presence of Jesus Christ in their lives, but by the specifically different thrust given to the Society by Ignatius Loyola and by the dynamism he capsulized in the Exercises, the Constitutions, and the rules.

To specify further is as difficult as it is for a man to give specific reasons why he loves and chooses one woman rather than another. To me, at least, the epitome is found in the word magis--"the more." The motto of the Jesuit is to seek "the greater glory of God." But how?

Perhaps an analogy can limp in the direction of clarification. The Jesuit, like the medical corpsman, is surrounded by an immense field of the wounded, the needy, the dying. No matter where he turns, his knowledge and training and skills are desperately needed. The screams and groans for help are everywhere and he responds with a passion. So far no difference from any other educated man, be he atheist or Christian, religious or lay. But the Jesuit believes that he has as it were a man on a hill whom he trusts has a better view of the entire carnage than he has, someone who can see where the greater need is, the greater hope of saving lives, especially the lives which are more valuable because they can rise up and help with the other wounded.

The superior is fallible. More than once he will mistakenly pick a man from one position where he is working relatively well and send him to an area of futility, both for him and for the people he has come to serve. But it is the Jesuit's last-resort conviction that the superior does have the widest view; more importantly, both superior and Jesuit believe that even when mistakes are made the mistakes are being used by a God who is not answerable to us. It is the core of the Jesuit's vow as a Jesuit that no matter how he stumbles or his superior stumbles, both are at the disposal of Jesus Christ--who is the ultimate Savior.

Perhaps the man is an excellent priest. Perhaps he is an excellent Christian. Perhaps he is an excellent worker. But if he is not basically with the rest of us, he is not a Jesuit. Let him do good work. Let him justifiably claim heroism. But let him not claim brotherhood in the Society that numbers the silent Teilhard de Chardin and the foolishly unpublished Hopkins. They have paid too much to belong to the Company to have their offering diluted by letting it encompass all good men who go their own ways.

Something in the meaning of the Society claims to be universal, to transcend even the heartfelt needs of the individual as he sees situations from his own hard-won bailiwick. I know. More than once I have fought and lost; more than once I have fought and won. The individual Jesuit must be "stretchable" enough, with such a love of God, that he will submit his life-long project to the will of the infallible Spirit as expressed in the judgments of a highly fallible superior. Ignatius capsulized it when he said that if the pope were to negate the Society, he could face it provided he had fifteen minutes of mental prayer. The first Jesuit knew best what being a Jesuit means.

To do less is to choose the "now" of the Church against the "forever" of the Church. To do less is to claim to be the all-seeing God. That is not the posture of even the minimal Jesuit; that is the posture of the enemy who says, "non serviam. "

Something at the core of true Jesuitness demands that a man worthy of the name and the claim submit his own choices to the will of the Spirit--even when the Spirit asks that he slay Isaac, the son of the promise.

Fish or cut bait.

The Close-up

Every Jesuit community has a personality of its own. Some are as large as 120 men, some as small as two. Some get a large part of their spirit and an added sense of unity from the college or high school all the members serve. Whereas in larger urban houses the community may be a mixed bag of teachers and administrators, parish priests, hospital chaplains, mission bureau personnel, students at nearby secular universities, foreign visitors.

The many divergences within the Society as a whole are intensified by compression. To be honest, there are large communities where Jesuits in cassocks, both old and young, gather in one corner of the recreation room, with the shirts and ties in another corner, and the sweat shirts and jeans in still another. Which leaves a fourth corner for the precarious, the peacemakers, and the promiscuous.

It is too facile to call this a "generation gap, " since there are bald heads and grey beards in each of the corners. It is more precisely a "mentality gap. " Some want to preserve the ways in which the Church and the Society have long embodied their congruent visions, and many of these men now feel "like strangers in the very houses they themselves have built. " Others are impatient even with the present speed-of-light rate of change, angered at our apparent slavery to the upper-middle class, intolerant of permanent commitment to landed institutions, and at times even intolerant of permanent commitment to the Society itself.

But these are caricatures trundled out by either side in an argument; they are rarely if ever realized in any one man or other. In most of the many communities I have seen in the United States, this kind of dramatic division occurs only in the few very large communities we have left, and many of those are even now being broken up by small groups forming satellite communities and by the natural process of old age.

The community I live in now is, I think, more or less typical. We have only nineteen men--three retired, a superior, a brother-minister, a rector-president, principal, three student counselors, a treasurer, a development director, a librarian, a special student in residence, and five full-time fighting braves. For the moment we have no scholastics.

The age-range runs from thirty to eighty. We work together, have drinks together, eat meals together, watch Friday horror movies together. There are men in the community who read only periodicals like Twin Circle; there are men who read only periodicals like The National Catholic Reporter; others read both; some read neither. There are men who light votive candles to Dan Berrigan and men who would hold the coats for his firing squad. And we really quarrel--but we do quarrel enough and openly enough to let off the steam that naturally builds up in all families. It keeps us growing, keeps us knowing one another better, keeps proving that we care.

If when I went to McQuaid in 1965 I had been allowed to go through the twelve hundred-odd names in the New York Province catalog and pick the twenty men I'd most like to share a community with, I doubt I would have picked more than two of the men I presently live with. Instead, they were chosen for me. And because we've cleaned out flooded basements together, washed dishes together for weeks because we didn't have kitchen help, worked with the same kids, griped at the same rectors, harried the same principals, and pulled in our collective belts to keep the sheriff away from our door, there isn't one of them who doesn't seem indispensible to me.

We have our problems, but the word "our" is more important than the word "problems."

The Jesuit "fits into" (and that must be carefully understood) this Company of men who are alive with the same spirit of Jesus, each in his unique way. Hence he does not resent the "fitting in" as restrictive of his own development as an individual. On the contrary, here is where he finds his true identity, serving Christ with the brethren.

The easement of the strong Jesuit diversities, methinks, is already being found in a greater open-mindedness than one had in the days when "the Jesuit thing" was more easily seen in external practices like common litanies and cassocks with rosaries attached. Those signs were dear to the hearts of many, but they were not essential. They are gone now and there is little likelihood that they will be replaced by new communal symbol-criteria.

By open-mindedness I do not mean, "You do your thing and I won't bother you." The most open mind is, after all, an empty head; and evasive tolerance merely leads to peaceful coexistence. By open-mindedness I mean an active willingness to probe, to give what we as novices called "the plus sign." It is what Ignatius describes in the Premise of the Exercises: "It should be presupposed that every good Christian ought to be more ready to give a good sense to a doubtful proposition of another than to condemn it; and if he cannot give a good sense to it, let him inquire how the other understands it."

The optimum Society is not two groups of regimentally conservative and uniformly liberal Jesuits, but rather the healthy balance and cross-feeding of a growing tradition in which the recognized strengths of each position compensate for the insanities of the other. If the Society ever lost the excitement of unified diversity that it has had for centuries, it would cease to exist as a separate entity. Whatever aliveness that was left would be absorbed into some body more vital than itself. The continuance of the Spirit is not ineluctably fused to the continuance of the Society of Jesus.

But I, for one, have no fears on that score. If I had, I would never have dared make this book as honest as I have tried to make it.

Since the young by their own definition are more flexible, it seems that the initiative for building bridges of understanding and love should be with them. The young men who come into the Society today are able by their patience, tact, and charm not only to set the world a bit more on fire but also to rekindle Jesuits who may think their own days of holy arson are behind them. Young Jesuits are realizing more and more that their vows are not only a commitment to Christ and to the Church but also to their brothers wherever they may be along the spectrum of diversity.

My hope that this is not merely a pipe dream or even a long-range projection was given strong substance by two ceremonies of young Jesuits taking their first vows. The ceremonies were three thousand miles apart, one in the Fordham University Chapel in New York City, the other in the chapel of the Jesuit novitiate in Santa Barbara, California. The first was in May, 1974, the second in August, 1974.

In both places the novices about to take their vows sat in the pews with their parents; our parents weren't even allowed at the vow Mass. The music was made not by a solitary organ and a Gregorian chant choir, but with new hymns written by Jesuits for guitars, trumpets, recorders, and drums. And the two chapels jumped! The vows were said in English and said aloud, whereas even our rector probably couldn't hear our Latin vows two feet away.

But they were exactly the same vows, taken with the same understanding and the same joyful trepidation to the same Christ through the same Society. And instead of the almost hushed-away manner of our vows, the two chapels were thronged, not only with families and friends but with seventy to a hundred concelebrating Jesuit priests at each Mass. There were young priests just ordained, priests bent over with age and arthritis, balding priests, bearded priests. Where it counted, there were no gaps--none. This was a celebration of the whole province! These were our new brothers, and men from all over the two states traveled miles to welcome them into the Company.

If that doesn't solidify a man's hopes, nothing can.

One more aspect of the vows at Santa Barbara caught me and stayed with me for days afterward: there I was, three thousand miles from home in another province with men I'd never met and whose new names were so numerous I couldn't remember more than a few of them--and yet I felt completely, unquestionably, warmly at home. At the vows, the dinner, the speeches, the party in the evening, I was one of them. They took it for granted. And so did I. Because we were Jesuits.

Over the last 430 years it has always been the ideal, and most often the reality, that the Society of Jesus be the light-armed cavalry of the Church. Where there have been crises, we have been there--not always alone, not always on the "right" side, sometimes even on both sides--but we have been there.

Crisis is the call of Christ to the Christian, especially to the professional Christian, the religious who has agreed to take up his cross daily and follow Jesus. To save his life he must risk it. Moreover, susceptability to crisis is embedded in the Society's motto which says we will go where the need is most intense simply because that is where the greater glory of God can emerge.

Well, if it's crisis you're looking for, come and take your pick. Choose your challenge. We have more than enough to go around.

The Obvious Needs

No one has a crystal ball that can focus what specific crises
the Jesuit priest will be called upon to grapple with in ten or
twenty or thirty years. Change is so rapid today that Jesuits
of the near future may be colonizing the moon or living under
the sea or rebuilding churches and schools from atomic rub-
ble. After all, who suspected twenty-five years ago that Jesuits
would be in Congress?

Wernher von Braun has said that in twenty-five years--
when most first-year novices will be my age--a world without
regular civilian space travel will be as hard to imagine as a
world without telephones would be for us. Others predict that
there will be few if any bodily organs which cannot be supplied
by artificial implants. The sociological distinctions between
males and females will have disappeared; perhaps even the
biological differences will be handled by test tubes.

How much longer can we live? How much faster can we go?
Whatever the problems there will be Jesuits--God willing--
among the men and women attempting to solve them, since it
is a principal duty of priests to lead and to teach people where
they are. For this reason a Jesuit, unlike most diocesan
clergy, is a "hyphenated-priest." He not only engages in
liturgical and counseling work, but he also has another job
which frequently takes up more of his time than explicitly
pastoral work. He can be a priest-teacher, a priest-seismolo-
gist, a priest-actor, a priest-almost-anything. Priest-astro-
nauts were in the works fifteen years ago. We have yet to have
priest-bellydancers but show us the need and give us a little
time.

In fact, as we have seen with the men described earlier,
this coordinate vocation is most often the Jesuit's entree to
the people. It is precisely because of his secular expertise
that his gospel message is less intimidating to his coworkers
and to the people he serves in his nonreligious work. He is,
as the cliché goes, "in the world but not of it." This adaptability itself could be a crisis for a Jesuit if he should make

himself so adaptable to his audience that he compromises the essentials of the gospels and of his vocation.

This hyphenation is ingrained in the Jesuit; and it is most likely that if the Society and the world survive, Jesuits will continue to have jobs other than the strictly ministerial. But what works will he hyphenate himself with? One rather sure bet is that no matter how long we live or how fast we go there will be Jesuits teaching in schools and colleges, perhaps a smaller percentage of our number in perhaps fewer institutions, but teaching is almost as natural to Jesuits as the Exercises.

Whether they are in a classroom or a lab or a sound studio, whether in Manresa or Melbourne or Mars, all Jesuits are inveterate apostles and, as such, all are crypto-teachers waiting to break open the Good News and explain it. Despite the bewildering number of different apostolates Jesuits now engage in as individuals and as groups, the major commitment of the Society as a whole in the United States has been to formal education. We operate at present in forty-nine high schools, ten colleges, and eighteen universities serving 250,000 students.

But with rising costs and consequent dependence on lay faculties, government grants, and lay boards of trustees our Jesuit colleges and universities are becoming less and less distinguishable from secular institutions. Because of dwindling vocations our high schools are staffed by fewer and fewer Jesuits and more and more laymen. Should we close down some of our schools and consolidate? Should we close them all and infiltrate elsewhere? Should we continue as many as we have and attempt to "Jesuitize" the lay faculties? Should we revolutionize our system and combine four years of high school and four years of college into six years of a move-at-your-own-pace combination school?

Whatever is done, it will be men ordained in the early 1980's who will make the decisions and make them grow.

But what will Jesuits be teaching in our schools or in somebody else's schools or on street corners or in taverns? Again God gives us no crystal ball, but he does give men of intelligence and prudent foresight. And courage. We can look at

the seeds of the present and prognosticate rather surely what
some of the major needs will be that will engage the minds
and hearts of the men who enter the Society today.

On the ground level the technological problems of our over-
populated, over-industrialized, over-urbanized planet are already becoming more immediate and more urgent. The practical need facing the priest-sociologist in the past was food
and shelter and jobs and dignity for the poor. Within the next
ten or twenty years this need could involve not only the poor but
what is now the middle class. Further, the problems of ecology,
law enforcement and penology, urban planning, equitable government, and innumerable social ills cry out for solutions today that cannot wait for too many tomorrows. The very planet
itself is a field alive with the need for hyphenated priests.

But below the ground level there is the need for priests to
minister to the hunger of the human mind and heart and spirit.
And that hunger is more profound and elusive than the pangs
of the belly. It is enormous and growing. It is the more and
more desperate need men and women have to feel like human
beings again. Other men can solve fuel shortages and balances
of payment and traffic jams. But as Dachau proved so dramat-
ically, a man can live with very little bread, indeed, provided
he has a reason to stay alive. It is this need that the priest is
ordained to serve.

Because of its presuppositions the "world" must treat all
such mysteries as problems, and the solutions it now offers
men's most human cravings are thin fare at best. For loneliness and self-hatred and alienation, there is TV, pills, pot,
booze, casual sex, and an increasing number of other forms
of slow and palliative suicide. For the need "to be somebody,
to be important, to count," there is the bank balance, the extra
car, the raise, the house at the lake; even ulcers can be worn
as a badge of success. For the need to belong to something bigger than oneself, there is the Elks, the Five-Year Plans,
Hell's Angels, the Myth of Progress. For the need for perma-
nence, the need to survive death, there is a choice of crema-

tion, quick-freezing, or the Cadillac hearse to the watertight burial vault.

All mysteries have been reduced to problems which, given enough time, are solvable.

And the ideal man is simplified to "The American Dream," a well-fed, well-muscled, soulless, and untroubled automaton.

If this doesn't cry out for priests, then the nation's youth are deaf and the gospels are dead.

The priest of today and tomorrow cannot, like Hans Brinker, hold back the entire tide of dehumanization by himself. He can, however, enkindle a small number of men with the hope of divinization which is the Good News. And the sparks from that number will spread here and there, with agonizing slowness perhaps, but inexorably. And it is the Jesuit's avowed purpose, after all, to spread fire on the earth.

The real problem beneath the surface dehumanization of mankind is at once so pervasive and so subtle that, like poisoned air, it is everywhere but unseen. What makes man human is being slowly, slowly sucked out of him. For reasons he cannot even fathom, he is being bribed to surrender whatever powers within him made him more than a beast, and without which he becomes a beast. His self. His soul.

And that is the call for the Jesuit of the 70's and 80's: to give man back his soul. Before it is too late.

The Real Enemy

It must have been far easier to be a Jesuit in the Age of the Reformation or in the Age of the Enlightenment. At least the sides must have been clearer. You knew, as the saying goes, "who the bastards were." They were the Protestants in the first case and the Philosophers in the second. With the Reformers four hundred years ago, the battle was over a Church that both sides thought important enough to save, important enough to change. With the Philosophers two hundred years ago, the struggle was over a Church both sides thought important, the Jesuits to save it and the Philosophers to uproot it. In those struggles you knew what they stood for and what you stood for. And the best part was that they hated Jesuits enough to make the Society the prime target for their attacks. To them, the Jesuits "were the bastards." However painful and prolonged, the antagonisms were clear, the adversaries were predictable.

But nowadays who thinks the Church is important enough to want to change it? Nowadays who thinks the Church is relevant enough to bother with the effort to destroy it?

Today and tomorrow the faceless, amorphous, disdainful enemy will not be antagonism but indifference.

A man can deal with an opponent who gives him the respect of despising him as the opposition. But how do you deal with an opponent who considers his case so secure and your opposition so irrelevant that you become no more than an occasional and very peripheral annoyance, like one fly in his manifesto?

Secularism is in the saddle, and barring a thermonuclear simplification, it is quite likely to stay there for generations.

Secularism, and its more palpable look-alike, materialism, and their academic triplet, logical positivism, were all born from the same conviction: that human knowledge is limited to what can be proved conclusively by the methods of science. Anything else will not compute and therefore is either non-existent or negligible.

One of the many midwives of these triplets was Rene Descartes who stated that one could accept as plausible only what he knew so clearly and distinctly that he could have no occasion to doubt it. The data of faith, then, not provable beyond doubt and in fact too elusive for scientific method, must be judged as beyond human comprehension and therefore beyond human concern.

There is nothing beyond explanation. All mysteries can be ultimately reduced to solvable problems.

The results have been legion. In a kind of delayed fruition, the Enlightenment had disposed of the Church by the simplest possible method, by making it inconsequential. If the pseudo-realities at the heart of the Church--God, salvation, Jesus, the afterlife--are by definition unreal, then one need waste no more time arguing about the Church.

There are repercussions of this basic assertion in society, and however much we doomsayers cry out against them, the ordinary man sees the immediate benefits to himself and finds the arguments against secularism so abstruse that he contents himself with the ice cream on his plate.

Knowledge, then, becomes no more than shrewdness, a practical means to man's only purpose in life: satisfying his immediate needs and desires. As W. H. Auden put it, "He has everything necessary to the Modern Man: a phonograph, a radio, a car, and a frigidaire." God, if he exists, turned his back on the whole thing long ago.

One needs only to look around to see how quietly and how thoroughly secularism has triumphed.

Students are encouraged to discover things for themselves, which is all well and good. But they fail to be shown that what we know only rarely results from personal discovery. For the most part what we know results from believing--textbooks, teachers, newspapers, doctors, television, and above all scientists. But not saints.

In a world conditioned since birth to immediate satisfaction or a money-back guarantee, faith becomes the height of naiveté. God? Who needs him? "I'll get by with a little help from my friends": pot, booze, pills, TV, and all the palliatives science can provide. Any talk of an intimate personal relationship between a believer and Christ is really a childish attempt to escape the confusions of life, clinging to the foot of an invisible six-foot rabbit.

Without a God who knows man's purpose for living, it must be the individual man himself who decides his personal purpose and the means to achieve it. Good and evil become real only insofar as they relate to his personally chosen goal. If I judge that slaughtering Jews is good, so be it. If you disagree, you'd better be tougher than I am. If I judge that covering up governmental injustice is a good, so be it. It may be illegal but it is not immoral. Whether it is political "misjudgments" or cheating on a test or sleeping with my girl, the only sin left is getting caught.

Along with sin, of course, one automatically jettisons any possibility of human dignity. If I cannot be blamed for my acts, neither can I be praised for them. There is no such thing as an evil act as long as I am both the defendant and the ultimate judge. If the society I belong to makes me feel guilty or rejected for what they call my antisocial behavior, the rejection is unjustifiable. I am, after all, no more than the complex product of my socialization, the product of my training and environment. If I misbehave, it is not I who am blameworthy, it is my innumerable programers.

And here is the ultimate dehumanization. I have lost my freedom to say that it is I who choose. I have lost my "I." I have lost my self. I have lost my soul.

And thus Dr. B. F. Skinner opens the antiseptic white doors to 1984.

If human beings become unlimitedly program-able, then it is the technicians, the men and women who can figure out the most efficient use of available hardware and "personnel," who will rule the earth. The euphemisms already abound: students become "educands," workers become "the labor force," human lives cut short by war before their prime become "casualties." Love becomes reducible to sex, sex is reducible to physical release, and man is reduced to a mass of chemicals and electricity, bagged in a hairless hide and . . . holding. A zombie.

And remember: the technological establishment has at least one little box in every American home quietly hypnotizing, brainwashing: "the more things you have, the happier you'll be . . . the more things you have, the hap- . . . ."

But something rebels.

So we have the flower children, trying to simplify, trying to find in the purity of natural things a power and resurrection. What they find is beautiful but still not big enough for man. Then, too, we have the drug users searching in ever more intense chemical highs for the ecstasy Teresa of Avila found in a bare cell. We have Yoga enthusiasts, sensitivity groups, the TM folk, who find islands of peace but no permanent home. Flowers are palpable, pills are palpable, bodies are palpable. But the Answer is not.

The harvest is ripe.

So the priest comes in all kinds of disguises, beads, cassocks, tweeds, and shouts and pleads that he has the Answer. But one feels at times ridiculous and often lonely, like the fundamentalist in the whorehouse shouting, "This really isn't the best fun, you know!"

On the "Today" show Barbara Walters leaned over to me during a commercial and said, "How can an intelligent man like you be a priest?" Which needs no comment.

To someone who knows the Old Testament, this apostolic situation is nothing new. For generation after generation from Noah through Isaiah to John the Baptist the prophets rose up against "a perverse generation which has gone a'whoring after the idols of Mammon." And their listeners sneered.

It is a lonely task for a man who has met in unfashionable silence and solitude the One who says, "I am Yahweh. I will free you of the burdens the Egyptians have laid upon you. . . . I will adopt you as my people, and I will be your God."

But the call, whenever or wherever it comes, is always the same as the call to Isaiah: "Whom shall I send? Who will be our messenger?"

And Isaiah says, "Here I am. Send me."

The greatest obstacle to a vocation today is, of course, everything that was said in the last chapter. If the priests already
in the Society are in some way tinged by secularism, it is legitimate to suspect that the young men in whom the Society
places its hope for vocations must also be affected by it. They
have, after all, been victims of the hypnotic little boxes longer
than we.

A young man today demands positive proof before committing
his life to the Society of Jesus. He has only one life to live, and
he surely is not going to hand it over without some assurance
that he is not giving it to a dying proposition. What's more,
adolescents fresh from the traumatizing discovery that their
once infallible parents and priests and presidents do make mistakes, are very wary of trust. If I had to isolate one of the
deepest fears a young man has today, it would be the fear of
being hoodwinked, fooled, being taken-advantage-of.

Whereas we treated our pastors as unquestionable oracles,
young men today give that uncritical acceptance to scientists.
And why not? Surely science has shown more palpable results

in alleviating the surface-level problems of mankind than the ploddingly cautious Church has. Not only has the Church been apparently irrelevant in the face of progress, but the voices within it no longer sing in undeviating chorus as they did twenty-five years ago. Now the answers offered by religious voices seem as contradictory and abrasive as the nonreligious voices. What's more, priests who were admired and even idolized, who preached chastity as a requirement of full manhood, have left their priesthood and their celibacy and quite often their Church behind them.

In flight from the tormenting complexity of today's world, a young man can be tempted into the simplification offered by an obedient consumerism. Or he may be tempted in the opposite direction by the hymns of Aquarian Rock into the simplification offered by romantic spontaneity. But he will not find much real joy or lasting fulfillment in either the system hero or in the flower child. The question is, of course, whether he will find it in priests--or at least more in priests than in anyone else.

Nowhere does the relativism and uncritical tolerance of today's secularism create more confusion than in the area of sex, which is a very recent and very volcanic discovery of a young man within himself. In my era the onslaught of puberty was exactly the same. No matter how many or how candid one's sex education courses, the real experiential knowledge so far outdistances the textbooks that it makes the two as different as the catechism and infused prayer. And it is always a battle with understanding that one fights alone.

Today, however, the world in which sexual maturity comes of age is far different from what it was. When I was in eighth grade, one had to sneak into the library's art books to see what a naked woman looked like. Today Hugh Hefner's candor is nearly passé and to some even puritannical. The young man who decides to be a Jesuit today must have a stronger conviction than I did, coming as he may from a co-ed college dorm where some fellow-students' roommates had no need of jocks.

Why should a man embrace celibacy when there are so many other more immediately satisfying things he can now safely embrace? Why should he deny himself a part of life that most men take for granted and some believe essential for total fulfillment? Why, indeed? Unless there is something even more essential.

College itself, ironically, is another deterrent to vocations --despite the fact that Jesuits perhaps get the best education available in the world. There is, to be sure, the wise choice of going to college before considering a vocation in order to achieve a fuller maturity, a clearer realization of the options, a more certain possession of oneself as a person. If one is to "lose his life for the Kingdom," he must certainly have a self to lose.

There are other reasons, though, less able to sustain scrutiny. There is the excitement of going to college; everyone else is going. There is also the feeling that college is a chance to prolong the comfortable dependencies of adolescence, but away from home. It provides a chance to delay decision not only about a priestly vocation but about any other vocation as well. This moratorium on commitment extends also to questions every man must face in order to attain his full manhood: his personal stance on money, cheating, sex, alcohol, belief in God, membership in the Church. To many it is as if maturity were not a gradual series of small struggles and small advances but a magic moment like the click of a psychological thermostat.

A few years ago the "in" thing seemed to be vocal radicalism. Today, only a few years later, it seems that a disillusioned passivity has set in. When everybody but the fanatic do-gooders and the Sammy Glicks is whiling away the hours in the Rathskeller, it's difficult to halt inertia and come to a decision. Especially a self-sacrificial decision.

Today all the visible props that sustained vocations in my day are either gone or merely endurable: the sodality, daily Mass, novenas, rosaries, May devotions. Much of it I admit was uncritical piosity, and I myself would probably wince with embarrassment to listen to a high school senior by a statue of our Lady at lunch hour extolling "The Tower of Ivory. " (And if that's an "in" joke, it shows how far we have come.)

But something more subtle is missing too--not just the mystique that surrounded the priest as a man of God, but the mystique of the liturgy itself which has lost its Latin and fancy trappings but has also lost its power in most cases to spellbind. In achieving intelligibility it seems also to have lost its meaning. Yesterday agnostics like Henry James could go into quiet paroxysms of delight over the beauty of the liturgy in Mont St. Michel--without once being grasped by its Truth. Today it takes a man with a faith which probes below surfaces to see and be gripped by the Truth we have come to celebrate at Mass.

There is still among young men in the Church today that same susceptibility to the unapparent, that same need for a meaning beyond death, that same anguish to open the eyes of the self-blinded, that same need to love more than one family, that same urge to give of himself, that same fascination with the Person and the deeds and the message of Jesus Christ that Ignatius felt as he lay broken at Loyola.

He is the man we want.

I got a letter recently from a student asking how someone could become a Jesuit. "Ever since the age of nine, I have admired priests," it said, "their dedication to the Church and to Jesus Christ, their effort to make him everyone's savior." So far, so good. It went on, "Now don't discriminate against me because I'm only in eighth grade; that isn't my fault. And don't discriminate against me because I'm female; that's not my fault either. I'm also not Catholic, but neither are Jesuits, or so I've heard."

Sorry, honey, but it's not my fault either.

At basis, anyone who wants to be a Jesuit has to be a Catholic male and at least a high school graduate. He should be a man of honest and open-eyed faith, reasonably intelligent, reasonably healthy physically and psychologically, sexually and spiritually. He should be mature enough to be fully aware that in entering the novitiate he is embarking on a two-year trial period that will conclude, if both sides are satisfied, with a definitive and permanent commitment of his life to chastity, poverty, and obedience in the Society of Jesus. He must have a sense of his own self-worth and of his manhood sufficient to understand that his offering of himself to God is a gift of real value. And that offering, free of illusions, should give him real inner peace and joy.

If that description sounds like the candidate has to be El Perfecto even before he applies, don't fret. They let me in, didn't they?

Most Catholic young men consider the priesthood at least remotely once or twice after their first communion. Most of them reject the idea for one reason or another. For others, though, the pesky impulse grows stronger until it begins to assume the proportions and the qualities of a real temptation. It creeps up periodically on such a man, provokes fascination at one time and revulsion at another, becomes all ensnarled with exhilaration and guilt and peace and turmoil. But then something comes up to distract him and, at least for awhile, he's free of the damn thing.

For a still smaller number the temptation begins to look pretty serious. It hangs on longer, leaves a warmer feeling, sometimes provokes daydreams or even a few experiments at writing one's name with "Rev." in front and "S.J." at the end. It begins to feel like falling in love with a girl you're rather sure you don't want to fall in love with.

"What the hell do I do now?"

Well, first of all, if you fit the description of the little girl in the first paragraph of this chapter, you'd better forget it-- at least till you become sixteen or a Catholic or a male. If you're okay so far, take a look at the description of El Perfecto in the third paragraph above. Again, it's not as inaccessible as it might seem. Most young men know themselves well enough that they can give at least a tentative judgment about their faith, their intelligence, and their health. It's the motives that become confusing at times, and at times too, the faith.

What follows may help to clarify those items. If it does, then the wisest thing to do is to leave the ultimate clarification to the process of admission and to the decision of God express-

ed by the provincial. It is the young man who, after soul-
searching and advice, proposes the marriage; but in the end
it is the young lady who says yes or no. .

And that metaphor is not a bad one to keep in mind since,
at least to me, falling in love is the only analogy that can
truly be used to describe a Christian's relationship with God.

Taking vows and being ordained are very much like getting
married. Holy orders and matrimony are both sacraments by
which the Church seals and celebrates a lifelong vocation.
And yet there are many people one loves without wanting to
marry them. So too there are many people who love God, but
not all of them "marry" him. The novitiate, then, is like an
engagement, a tentative commitment to test the relationship,
to find out more about one another, to reflect with serious-
ness whether this really is the way I can most fully and richly
live the one life I have. The question now, though, is whether
one even wants to get engaged.

The best criterion of a good decision, and we will return
to this again, is whether it gives a prolonged and profound
sense of peace and freedom. But not every sort of peace is
the peace of Christ, the peace he wished his apostles. The
feeling of relief and freedom a man experiences when he dumps
a heavy burden of responsibility or when he finally gets what
he's craved for a long time, is not necessarily the peace that
underlines the Truth, the peace that signals the will of God.

A man might feel relief at finding something to occupy his
life after a heartbreaking split from "the only girl for me,
ever. " Another man might be consoled by feeling he has finally escaped into a sanctuary away from women, with all their
threats to his virtue and all the guilt feelings they call forth.
Or he might feel the deceptive peace of finally getting his
mother off his back, with her incessant rosaries and her
plaintive looks that crave "a priest in the family. " There is
a certain comfort, too, in thinking one has found security-
with-honor away from the responsibilities of ordinary adult
life to which one doesn't feel quite equal. The religious life
could also be simply a high-toned escape from insoluble per-

sonal problems, a sort of lifelong clerical pill bottle. Nor is it unheard of that a man enter the seminary sheerly to atone for his sins or to punish himself.

Neither the priesthood nor marriage ought to be used as a life-filler or a reluctant settlement or a psychiatrist's office. Both are calls to well-balanced people to become creators.

A true vocation can be judged by the length and depth of the peace it gives and by the willingness of the man to be utterly open in sharing his feelings and himself with a wise advisor.

This is not to say, however, that the peace of the true vocation is uninterrupted. Unless a man feels some resistance to giving up wife and children, financial advancement and complete independence, he very likely doesn't really know what he's doing. Those things are pretty damned beautiful! If they weren't, the offering of the vows would be inconsequential and ultimately meaningless.

The gospel, after all, goes against the grain of the value system engendered in a boy since birth. The cult of competition has infected him perhaps more than he realized: report cards, athletics, family rivalries, CEEB's, parents' expectations, and so on. The world cheers, "We're #1! We're #1!" And Christ says, "If you want the first place, take the last place." If there isn't some resistance to letting oneself go, there might be very little self to offer.

Despite what's been said, the Society does not expect prefabricated little Ignatius Loyolas turning up at the novitiate merely waiting for the Good Housekeeping Seal of Approval at vows. Ignatius himself had a lot to learn when he set out on his journey as the first Jesuit. Every man who follows him has a lot to learn too, a lot of growing to do, a lot of mistakes to make, a lot of potholes to be filled in.

So, presuming that a man and his advisor give him at least pretty good marks for the faith, the intelligence, the health, the motives, and the peace--how does he know?

This section will be comparatively brief; first, because most
young men have a fairly good idea of what a priest is and,
second, because the description has already been written better than I could hope to write it. I would refer the reader to
the Epistle to the Hebrews. But here are my own thoughts.

The priest is, at least as far as his limitations allow, another Christ: trustworthy, compassionate, self-sacrificial.
It is his task to shake men out of their slaveries to the mas-
ochism of self-pity and to the unloving conformism of the law.
It is his task to awaken men to the freedom of the sons of God.
Like Christ he is to stand at the altar, in the pulpit, on the
street, in the fields, as a mediator between the Father and
mankind, moving easily between two worlds, to bind up the
wounds of sin, to cast out devilish self-doubts, to raise men
from the death of sterile comfort. And "it is not as if we had
a High Priest who was incapable of feeling our weaknesses
with us; but we have one who has been tempted in every way
that we are."

Most visibly, the priest offers Mass, the sacrifice of man-
united-to-God. And if he does, by God, let him celebrate it
in a way that his fellow Christians can see and feel that for
him it is a celebration of our Brother's victory over death.
When the priest says, "this is my body which will be given up
for you" and "this is my blood . . . to be shed for you and for
all men so that sins may be forgiven," let him mean it not
only of the scapegoat Christ but also of himself. At least let
him try.

One day in an elevator in Toronto, a priest happened to
realize that the man with whom he shared the elevator was
Groucho Marx. With a little throat clearing, he overcame his
embarrassment and said to Groucho, "Mr. Marx, I don't
mean to intrude, but I want to thank you for all the joy you've
shared with your fellowmen." Without missing a beat, Groucho
looked up and said, "I wish I could say the same for you fellas."

When Claire Booth Luce was thinking of becoming a Catholic, she says she found herself looking at men in Roman collars and saying to them inside herself, "You say you have the truth. Well, the truth should set you free, bring you alive, give you joy. Can I see your joy?"

The priest is a professional Christian, and like the Father whose name he tries to be worthy of, the priest is always "on call." If the Christian's vocation is to be used up, even by people unworthy of his gift, the priest signs on to be a professional at it. He is the leader who has to keep his people going even when everybody else wants to give up, including himself. I'm reminded of a weekend I was helping out in a parish. It was the week Jack Kennedy was assassinated, and the phone rang and rang and rang. As he went over to answer it for the hundredth time, the young curate looked at me with a wry smile and said, "Ya wanna know why priests leap the league?" He pointed to the telephone. "That."

All that sounds pretty frightening, but so is Christianity. One does his best, which often seems not quite good enough, even though God might think so. Let me confess that the reasons for including these paragraphs with their quite intimidating and probably unrealizable ideal of the priestly vocation is merely to test how serious a man is. Entering the novitiate is not quite the same as signing aboard The Pequod.

"Why do you want to be a priest?" When I answered that question on my application for the Society, I put down "to save my soul and the souls of others." I suppose somebody told me to say that, or I read it somewhere and thought it would impress the hell out of the provincial. Every other applicant probably wrote exactly the same thing. I really entered with a goal far foggier than that. I wanted to be like the Jesuits I knew, whatever that meant. I'm sure I really believed that business about souls then, and I surely believe it now. But I've only recently begun to understand what those words "save" and "soul" truly mean.

As I said before, Ignatius was looking for heroes, men willing to endure the poverty and the shame of Christ. But all men are not heroes at first. If a man were not sure about his heroic potential, Ignatius was satisfied with at least the desire to <u>want</u> to want heroism. As the father of the demoniac boy in the gospel said so beautifully, so humanly, "I believe . . . help my unbelief."

Remotely potential heroes will do.

Do You Want To Be a Religious Priest?

Diocesan priests do good work, and they do it at the only points where the lives of most Catholics touch the Church at all: Sunday Mass, baptisms, weddings, sick calls, and funerals. Why take on the added commitment of the three vows of religion?

Chastity

The vow of chastity, as Ignatius puts it with distressing terseness, "needs no explanation since it is evident how perfectly it should be preserved." It was also said that a Jesuit ought to imitate the chastity of the angels--a difficult task, methinks, since the angels, having no bodies or hands or sexual apparatus, must have a considerably easier job with chastity than men do. If a novice thinks he can live in the world without temptation or without the need for an occasional serious confession, he had better seek elsewhere. We are not worthy of him.

The vow of chastity, of course, goes beyond the virtue all Christians are called on to pursue. It is a vow of celibacy-- which all priests take--to give up forever the physical fulfillment of sex and the human fulfillment of sharing his life fully with another person and having children who are his own. It is not, by God, a surrender of his sexuality. He is male before and after his vow, and his fatherhood of other men's

191

children must be both tender and virile. Nor, by God, does he give up love to serve at some safe, aloof, and sterile distance, like a eunuch in a harem. It is precisely love--even a passion if you will--which motivates his celibacy, an unfeigned affection for his neighbors and an uncritical devotion to their Savior. If he is not alive with love, he is not a full Christian, much less a professional one.

The vow is an assertion that self-sacrifice is an even greater manifestation of love than sex is. Lest that statement seem naive or self-delusive, perhaps a story can clarify it. When I was born, it was a breach birth; and my mother was so torn by it that the doctor told my father to stay out of bed with her for about three months. He stayed away for a year rather than take even the slightest chance of hurting her in any way. Which way did he show more love, by sharing a bed with her or by sacrificing it? If the answer is not obvious, read no further.

But in the ordinary run of things men get married, celebrate and renew that sacramental gift by sexual intercourse, and have children who sadden and gladden their days and carry on their names to the tenth generation.

Why vow it away?

As with all the vows, the vow of celibacy is taken first in imitation of Christ who was unmarried, but it is also taken to make one freer to serve.

It has often been said that one can be married and still be free to serve. This is unarguable. Whether one can serve better or more freely as a celibate is open to debate. Without denigrating the service of married Christians--not the least of whom are the men and women I have worked with as a fellow teacher--I still say that celibacy makes me freer. If it didn't, I'd be out there practicing birth control with the rest, but in a far less total way than now!

If the pope were to abrogate celibacy as a requirement for the priesthood tomorrow, I would remain celibate. I assume that if that day ever came, there would still be religious priests who voluntarily assumed celibacy, not because marriage is a less worthy state but because it is not the best way for them to serve God.

Remember, then, that I speak for my own celibacy. Other men may have other reasons, some similar, some quite different. These are mine.

I figure that I have a certain scope and intensity in my ability to love. I admit that love is not a finite, quantifiable substance; it is rather a spiritual power. But as with all human powers, it is limited by the individual's limitations--my threshold of fatigue, the time in a day, my predelictions for some people over others. I have just so much love that I can give, but I want to love--really love--as many people as I can with the same intensity of love that I would give to the woman of my dreams and the children of my loins. For me, one family is not enough. Lest that seem condescending, let me explain.

If I were married, I would feel that my family deserved a large measure of my "best" power to love and a large measure of my "best" time. Others, perhaps, can serve the people they work for at full intensity and then go home and give their families the same fullness of themselves. I can't, and I don't know many people who can. I have, in fact, had more experience of the contrary. I know politicians, doctors, researchers, entertainers, and community servants who selflessly devote enormous amounts of time and energy to the service of their fellowmen. And they furthered their own careers only insofar as they could improve their service to others. But their children are most often wretched. As my mother used to say, "The cobbler's children never have any shoes."

What's more, I have seen unmarried laymen in our schools labor without watching the clock for the boys they taught. They were available till all hours, off on a jaunt with a gaggle of kids weekend after weekend, completely at the behest of their students. They were our Mr. Chipses; Charlie Winans at Brooklyn Prep was one, Bob Bradley at McQuaid was another. But when Bob Bradley was married and began to have children, even though his wife shared his enthusiasm for the school and the boys, he couldn't give the same time, the same total intensity of his loving and working to his students. He had to focus a significant part of his "best" self on the four people who were his in a way that they were nobody else's.

I, on the other hand, have freely chosen to keep my power to love "unfocused. "

Whatever I have to give of love is there, waiting, for anyone who needs it, and no one--not my wife or my children--not my mother or my sister or her children--has a prior claim on me. It sounds harsh to some, but no more harsh than leaving Nazareth for Jerusalem to be about one's Father's business. Whoever comes along has whatever I have to give, for as long as he or she needs it, even though they don't deserve it, even though I find it difficult to give.

This is an ideal and I have failed it more than once in many kinds of ways. But I don't want to go on in any other way. At times my celibacy has been a difficult gift to offer. But as soon as it becomes negligible, it will cease to be a gift.

There is another aspect of celibacy I have discovered only recently and, although it is most definitely a peripheral advantage, it is nonetheless interesting. Very often when I am with truly good "worldly" people--and I have been quite often, at parties, in plays, in secular schools, in the movie--one question invariably comes up once we've gotten to know and trust one another. And I mean invariably. The question always comes in the same forthright, earthy form: "Bill, tell me one thing--honest; do you mean you've never gotten laid?"

It's understandable, I suppose. I'm a good man. I am not so ugly that small children scream at my approach. I can drink and tell blue jokes with the best of them. I don't cower in a corner or pull out the exorcist's manual when the talk gets rough or bitter or embarrassing. I'm just like they are, except for two things. In many cases, inexplicably, I am one helluva lot happier and more alive and more at peace than they are. And I'm celibate. How can I be happy when I've freely given up the one thing most of them consider the most important part of their lives? To them I am one exasperating enigma.

"Why?" they ask. And I tell them, just as I have here.

Thus, just as whatever nonreligious expertise I have gives me an entree for the gospel, so--paradoxically--the seeming contradiction of my joy and celibacy gives me still another opening. The reason for my celibacy and my joy are the same: Jesus Christ.

I became celibate because the Society required it of me; I remain celibate because I require it of me.

Poverty

A diocesan priest can have his own car, a bank account, a second home in the country; a religious cannot. That doesn't make the religious some big-deal martyr or better than the diocesan priest. It merely means that a religious feels he can reach his individual goal much better without the encumbrances and comforts--and the responsibility--of money.

The vow of poverty means, quite simply, that a religious doesn't own anything. Nothing. He depends completely on the community for everything, and any money he receives--salaries, gifts, royalties, stipends, bequests: the works--all goes into the common pot. Anything he or any other member of the community needs comes out of that common pot. What's left over goes to the apostolates of the Society.

For instance, if I were a layman at my high school with my degrees and experience, I'd probably be making about $13,000 a year plus maybe $1,500 or $2,000 for giving talks and writing articles. When you divide the expenses of my community by the nineteen men in it, my "share" comes to about $3,500; the other $11,000 goes back into the school. The royalties from my theology book go to the province fund for supporting our seminarians while they are studying. It is, as it were, a "familial communism."

From the moment he walks in the door of the novitiate to the moment he's lowered into his grave, the Jesuit doesn't pay a cent for his education, his room and board, his beer, his shoelaces. Well, not quite. Actually he pays every cent he makes.

It sounds pretty easy, huh? At least it does to the kids at McQuaid when they see the beer truck pull up on what they believe is an hourly schedule. Yeah, I suppose two beers is a fair wage for a twelve-hour day.

I have often wished we could get enough Jesuits in my community--including my slovenly self--to clean up their rooms enough so that we could lead seniors goggle-eyed through our little palazzo. There are two rugs in the house, one in the rec room (after twenty years) and one in the chapel. The rest is a vinyl paradise. We have one seventy-year-old cleaning man who comes in twice a week to jiggle a dust mop in most of the open spaces. If aesthetics did not induce me to clean my sink every month or two, self-defense would, since frogs and toads could spontaneously generate therein at any given moment. (Chauvinist though it be, it's nice to have a mother or a wife who does your laundry.) Each of us lives in what is to all intents an office with a bed and a sink in it. The meals are ordinary, but nobody starves. There are better houses in the province; there are poorer houses. Nobody seems to mind, really. We all have more important things to worry about.

On the practical level, ours is a poverty of inconvenience --getting permissions, going on the cheap, and above all "making do." It's by no means a poverty of indigence; perhaps it should be closer to that.

But the deeper poverty is the poverty of advancement. Like the vow of chastity, it makes a man look like a fool even to the kindest worldling, since in the secular world sex and money are the two ways by which a man "makes his mark." As the poster says, "Money may not be everything, but it sure as hell beats whatever's in second place!"

Enough has been said in these pages about how men in our society define their personal value in terms of competition-- getting ahead of the other guy or at least not falling behind, getting the raise, getting the extra car, getting the kids into the college they want, and on and on. And men are accus-

tomed to define others' values in terms of salary too: Joe
Namath is important, teachers of braille are not; Nelson
Rockefeller is important, community organizers are not.
With the mind-set of the secular world, Jesuits may be very
smart, they may work very hard, but really . . . ya know
. . . what are they worth?

Less crassly, in the ordinary run of things a man gets a
job, and his paycheck is a symbol, it is a gift to his wife and
family, to feed and clothe and educate and entertain them.
For many a man, it's very difficult; but overcoming the difficulties is the road to his sense of self, his achievement,
his manhood.

I don't think it's arrogant to say that--even with my limited
talents, my limited experience, my limited mind--my un-
limited brashness and I could probably be making conservative-
ly $20,000 at this stage, with all that that figure connotes. But
I choose to live on $3,500. Why?

Why vow it away?

Again, the religious is poor primarily because Christ was
poor and still is poor in his people all over the world. But
one can also see, perhaps more readily than with chastity,
how poverty frees a man to serve.

I have often wondered, just for the fun of it, what I would
take out of my room if there were a fire. There are senti-
mental things which couldn't be replaced: the wooden Don
Quixote the cast gave me after "Man of La Mancha," the uni-
corn with the broken horn Mark Hanna gave me after I was in
"The Glass Menagerie," the Shalom plaque John Edelman gave
me when he came into the Society. But I always say to myself that I'd take my electric typewriter. Not that it couldn't
be replaced; not that it even has much trade-in value any
more; it grumbles and shudders like an old dray horse. But
we've hacked out a lot of stencils for high school kids and fed
a lot of novices together. My typewriter is a symbol to me of
what I do best.

But actually there's nothing that can't be replaced with a
little work or a little genial begging. Except the other Jesuits

in the house. Like any other member of a family, I'm rather
sure I'd get them out first, even if I had to leave Don Quixote
and my typewriter behind.

I truly think there's nothing physical in my life that I couldn't
leave behind, even--and it costs me to say it--McQuaid High
School. There's no bank account to build and protect, no treasure that moth or rust could eat. I don't have to watch the stock
market or the food prices; we have a treasurer and a minister
--poor men!--whose job that is. And their taking those jobs
leaves me free to teach, to preach, to talk, to act, to do what
I do best, showing off, for Christ's sake.

One more thing, specifically about my life at McQuaid, which
might shed some light on the paradoxical richness of poverty.
For the nine years I have been there we have teetered on the
brink of closure either from our creditors for nonpayment or
from the province which, understandably, had to think of the
greater potential for the glory of God in other works which
were crying for men. Oddly, it was our very poverty which
saved us--as a community. We had to do without. We had to
wash cars and dishes and johns because we couldn't afford
help. We had to pinch pennies until Lincoln was ready to re-
nege on the Civil War. But we pulled together. No matter what
our different points of view on politics or the training of Jesuits
or the way to teach boys, one thing united us: we were going to
save that school. It's amazing how many seemingly ugly people begin to look beautiful when you're bailing out a life raft
together.

Poverty like chastity also has the peripheral value of contradiction. Good "worldly" people look at religious who are
intelligent and talented and they wonder why the hell they waste
their time in soup kitchens and prisons and leper colonies. And
perhaps they find the answer.

There are individual Jesuits and some Jesuit communities
that seem to be living too well for poor men. If so, they don't
know what they're missing. No one can tell me--and surely
no one can tell a missionary--that shared poverty with a com-

mon will to survive is not creative of unity, of barrier-breaking, of love. One need only try it to see.

Obedience

For all the talk of total freedom today, there is no such thing--for anybody. No one is free, for example, of the law of gravity or the previous years of his experience or his height or his race or his fears. Nor is anyone who loves totally free; he has freely surrendered a claim on his freedom to those he loves. Anyone who takes a job freely surrenders forty hours of his week to someone else for money, someone who can tell him when to get to work, when to break for coffee, for lunch, when he can go home. The better-paying jobs can even tell him what to wear, whether he can sport a beard, who his friends ought to be, how much he can drink, where he will live. Compared to a Xerox executive who can be switched from Connecticut to L. A. to London--with his family--within five years, the Jesuit has a vow of rock-bound stability!

None of the vows has been so overdramatized and therefore so falsified as the vow of obedience. Such tales as the one in The Nun's Story, where the sister is commanded to fail her examinations for the sake of her humility, happen only in the pages of novels and on the big old silver screen. But how to convince even our admirers that we are not grim stoics manipulated like pawns by unfeeling fuehrers? Certainly in my quarter century as a Jesuit I have acquiesced in decisions of superiors which I thought were unjust. More often, far more often recently, I have seen superiors bend over double to be sure they heard all sides at least five times. In fact if I have any gripe now, it's with the delay in choosing options. The fascist in me keeps saying, "Whatever the decision, let's get on with it!" But I was not always that way.

Even today the Society is not a participative democracy. The superior takes counsel and the superior acts. If a man feels he has been misunderstood, he is not only allowed but nearly forced by rule to "represent," to explain once again to the superior what he meant in the hope that the misunderstanding was not about the objective value of his plan but about the Jesuit's failure to express it clearly enough. But when the superior says, "This," it's this.

Surely the obedience of the Society is easier, more flexible, more humane than the paid obedience of the efficient modern corporation.

The question "why" to this vow seems jejune. If you want to run a provincial operation with a thousand men, somebody's got to be in charge. On the other hand, if you want to work on your own, without the shackles of organized cooperation, then the world is yours to work in. If, however, you want to be part of a larger and potentially more effective organization, some pet projects and peeves have to give. Either we all win together or no one wins at all--including the People of God.

The "why" of obedience becomes more real to me when I try to envision what I'd say if my provincial, whom I happen to love as a friend and respect as a wise man, said to me, "Okay, Bill. Nine years at McQuaid is enough. Time for a change." I love McQuaid, the students, the parents, the faculty, my friends with all my promiscuous heart. What's more I've fought for it, and I have the same feeling that Ricci had for his Mandarins and Brebeuf had for his Hurons. Don't tell me their's was greater. It was not.

But if my provincial told me to go to another high school, to a parish, to retreat work, to the missions, I would go.

I would fight it. Boy, would I fight it, ploy and counterploy, bribe and threat, tooth and nail! But if he said, "That's it," I would go.

Why?

Well first because I was ordained for Christ and for my brothers, not just for the ones I have now or the ones I have grown comfortable with. Christ and my brothers are everywhere, in Rochester or Rio or Reykjavik. Also, I've been blessed by God and Jim Whedbee with the ability to love with shameless ease, and there is no geographical boundary to the

need for love and being loved. But, at bottom, the reason would
be that over the last twenty-five years my faith has grown.
I've obeyed superiors even when I knew they were wrong, and
yet from that (at times bitter) acceptance has come a growth
I could neither have planned nor expected. They were so
wrong in the short run and so unforeseeably right in the long
run, that I can't help but suspect a Conspiracy behind them.

All the Vows

   The basic reason for all three vows is to be like Christ, unmarried, without the restriction of goods, open to the voice
of the Father. The word "paradoxically" has been scattered
throughout these pages because paradox is at the root of human and Christian fulfillment: the more one gives up, the
more he is enriched. One only has to try it to find that out.
To be vowed as a religious is to be married to Christ; but if
all men and women are Christ's brothers and sisters, then
the religious has married into a very large family indeed. And
if it is true that Christ is somehow in every man and woman
I meet, I am--God help me--married to every man and woman
I meet, no matter how pleasant or unpromising, with all the
richness and responsibility that entails.
   There are Jesuits who flirt with and succumb to unchastity;
I have been one of them. There are men who compromise too
easily with poverty and grow content with their compromises;
I have been one of them. There are men who wangle their way
around the wishes of superiors, Jesuitically juggling words
and hiding behind bombast; I have been one of them.
   But for myself, I can only answer with the first pope who
bumbled a bit himself, "Lord, to whom else can we go? You
have the words of eternal life. "

Wow! If I haven't juggled with that one in the last two hundred pages, I ought to go back to square one!

If a young man really wants, as Ignatius says, "to distinguish himself in whatever concerns the service of the Eternal King," why should he consider saddling himself with the Society of Jesus, with all its turmoil, with all its disparate voices, with uncertainty on one side and complacency on the other, with men leaving, with smaller numbers entering--the lot?

I have tried to show that the Society today despite its limitations and problems is recognizably the same as the one Ignatius began on Montmartre 450 years ago. Further, what the Society is today is not irreparably far from what the young man thinks it ought to be--or from what either the radical or the reactionary Jesuit thinks it ought to be. The final questions remain for the young man himself to decide: is this an authentic means of giving one's life to Christ? And, is this the one I want?

How does the Jesuit order differ from other orders? In answering this question I have to ask the reader's indulgence since much of what follows will merely regroup what has gone before. This whole book has been an attempt to suggest an answer to that question.

First, all Jesuits have a common and specific spiritual heritage in the Spiritual Exercises which each one makes fully twice in his life and refreshes every year in his eight-day retreat. This heritage is concretized in the Constitutions of the Society which each Jesuit personally ratifies with perpetual vows.

Second, as a response to the call of the King in the Exercises, the Jesuit dedicates himself to searching out the magis, not the impossible dream of Don Quixote but, more practically, the scarcely possible dream. He searches in prayer to discern where the needs are greatest and how God wishes to use him. Then he goes.

Third, the Jesuit's quest for the expansion of God's kingdom is not done in the quiet of the cloister. The Jesuit has no office to chant in common, no obligatory penances, no unbending daily order. He is out in the world with little more than his training, his prayer, and his nightly return to the community to keep him from becoming as infected with secularism as anybody else. But as a hyphenated-priest he is where the need is, working with workers as a fellow worker--but with a message, waiting for the propitious time.

Fourth, because he brings the gospel to all kinds of men and women, he must be adaptable, as Jesus was when he spoke both to Peter the fisherman and Nicodemus the clergyman, as de Nobili was when he spoke to Brahmins by day and to Pariahs at night. The Jesuit must be adaptable in his time schedule, his clothing, his language, and above all in his approach to his audience. He is to be, insofar as he is able, "all things to all men. "

This adaptation requires tolerance, which is why the Jesuit training emphasizes the study of Christian humanism. The Jesuit has studied the great spectrum of human concern opened for him in the hundreds of seemingly impractical courses from atomic physics to Hebrew to statistics to yoga. He has studied the nearly infinite ways in which men all over the world for centuries upon centuries have looked at their God.

Because he has seen the basic goodness hidden in so many unpromising men, the Jesuit stands on the side of leniency if there is even the slightest evidence to justify leniency. It is for this reason that we have been singled out by Puritans, Calvinists, and Jansenists as the ungodly pushovers who spare the rod and spoil the child. But with the liberating insight of the Exercises, a Jesuit is inclined to resist the imposition of an obligation which is not certain and to give the best interpretation possible to any speaker.

This tolerance and leniency affect the composition of our own ranks, and the Jesuit must learn that difference of opinion, even within the brotherhood, even when it is painful, is the only way human knowledge advances toward the Truth. It is for this reason we must rejoice that we have both Drinan and McLaughlin, both Berrigan and Lyons, to check their excesses and ours, to rouse us to rethink and to grow. As Time said in its Jesuit issue, Father Arrupe "is not a man who takes more than reasonable risks. But he lets others move imaginatively in new directions, then defends and protects them. He does that, suggest some of his fellow Jesuits, because he looks to the victory of the Resurrection where many others are only able to see the defeat of Golgotha. In Christian life, however, the two are inextricably joined--in few places more so than in the Society of Jesus. "

Fifth, however hidden it may seem at times, the hallmark of the Jesuit has always been obedience. Even though, as many complain, the Society's mobility is compromised by so many landed institutions, the individual Jesuit's mobility is not compromised so long as he is obedient and the superior can move him without uproar from one institution or work to another wherever he sees the greatest need. And obedience gives us a unity and stability, a sense of belonging and a sense of continuity.

Sixth, a Jesuit is a man with a rich history of men ahead of him who amplify his sense of Jesuitness, point the way to the works and struggles he might encounter, and give him the courage of their example. They too have failed and triumphed; they too have felt helpless yet did great things in Him who strengthened them. He has Ignatius, Xavier, Jogues and Marquette, the Jesuits of the Reductions and the Jesuits of the Suppression, Hopkins and Pro and Dan Lord, Ciszek and Teilhard, and all the unknown greatnesses who help a Jesuit's vocation grow.

Make no mistake about it: if a man wants to be used, we will use him. And the being used will give him joy.

There are only two steps left: the proposal, which is an act of faith, and the response, which is also an act of faith, but shared.

When a young man reaches the age of seventeen, nineteen, or twenty-one, he has the opportunity to freely ratify the faith he submitted to from the unwitting baptism at birth to the unwilling church attendance in adolescence. He is capable now of understanding and weighing the claims of atheism and theism and choosing for himself whether he will believe or not. He can never be utterly certain, never have "evidence so clear and distinct that he can have no occasion to doubt it. " Like a jury in a trial, all he can hope for either way is a high degree of probability, a verdict "with no reasonable doubt. " He has calculated the evidence for and against; he has taken the risk and built his life on that calculated risk. It is his act of faith.

The decision about a vocation is no different except that it deals with a deeper commitment. It, too, is an act of faith. It is a calculated risk--and both terms are important.

The basic questions for the calculation part have been laid out, perhaps sketchily, in the preceding pages. But Father Vince O'Flaherty, a former master of novices, cautions that a decision to join the Society of Jesus "is not simply a matter of weighing pros and cons. A man's life is at stake. And men do not make choices affecting their destinies on the basis of detached prudential judgments. The whole of a man, and not simply his power of reasoning, is necessarily brought into play when the question is: What shall I make of my life?"

Just as with the faith decision of choosing to be a Catholic or not, and just as with the faith decision of becoming engaged or not, the faith decision of choosing to apply to the Society takes more than columns of pros and cons, although they certainly help to clarify the alternatives. But in all three cases, logic takes a man only so far. It takes a great deal of honest prayer with the One who calls and at least some candid discussion about that prayer with an advisor the man trusts.

Even then, although the man has made the calculation, although he is willing to take the risk, it is God's acceptance of the offer which is the gift of faith fulfilled. In the story of my own vocation Paddy Cummings and Ed Nagle and Jim Whedbee and so many others led me to the pump, but on that hill at Holy Cross and in that room at Woodstock it was Someone Else who shattered me with his acceptance. And only then, in both cases, did the Society of Jesus ratify that acceptance by admitting me as a novice, by allowing me first vows, by approving me for ordination.

Ignatius has written that in his struggle to come to a decision a man will experience moments of "interior peace, spiritual joy, hope, faith, love, tears, elevation of mind." But he will also experience moments of "conflict instead of peace, sadness instead of spiritual joy, hope in earthly things instead of hope in the higher, earthly love instead of spiritual . . . his mind wandering to base things rather than being lifted up."

It happened in Ignatius' decision; it happened in my own. And I have no doubt that it happened in every vocation between those two and that it will happen in every one to come. For this reason a man considering a vocation must have a wise advisor who can help him discern whether the occasional revulsion is an indication of God's testing or an indication that there is no vocation there at all.

The ultimate test is that a right decision gives an authentic sense of peace, a peace tested by time and by honest sharing with an advisor. It is a peace that involves "a real surrender of oneself, of all ambitions, fears, desires, attachments, that would keep the man from placing himself at God's disposal." If after the calculation, the prayer, and the advice, the young man can still say, "For me, to serve Christ is to enter the Society of Jesus, if the Society will have me"; then, holding his self vulnerably in his hands, it is time to offer himself. It is time to propose.

The Second Act of Faith

The first step for such a man is to contact the provincial in his area (see page 213) or to ask a Jesuit to do it for him. It's as easy as asking for a college application. Then the provincial will contact him and tell him what the rest of the admissions process is.

Even if it is not part of the admissions process in a particular province, it's a good idea to ask a Jesuit to write the novice director and see if there is a weekend the man can visit the novitiate, shoot the breeze with the novices, and see--secondhand but close-up--what novitiate life is like. All of the American novitiates take these visits for granted. They charge nothing. There's no feeling on either side that the man is committing himself to enter--just looking. A visit like this is not a bad idea even when the man has not yet applied for admission.

Allow me to give a bit of practical Dutch-uncle advice for the time after application as the interviews and testing drag on. First, keep checking in with the advisor you have trusted with your attempt to discern the vocation. The process is long and at times tedious; what's worse, the decision and the dream are so heady, so invigorating, so alive, that the process of repeating the same story over and over may seem to demean it, make it common or even boring.

Also, don't broadcast it. You may want to share all the bigness you feel with such a decision, but don't. First of all, you may be turned down; and then you'll have to endure the real or imagined pity of your peers. Secondly, broadcasting the message that "I'm going to be a Jesuit," jeopardizes your freedom to change your mind. Thirdly, it's been my experience that young men who announce their intentions before they're accepted begin to be treated like spun glass by their friends who fear to involve them in anything that might compromise their friend's "holiness." They are sometimes not asked to parties or proms by girls. They themselves begin to pontificate as if they were already invested as full-fledged gurus. In short, such men deprive themselves of the fullness and richness of student life that should be theirs. As that wise Jesuit told me, "Don't become a novice till you walk in the door."

Once the process of application is completed, you wait. And there's no way round it: it's an edgy wait. And the only wise way to fill the time is to keep busy, and when the demonic voices begin wondering about the outcome, resolve that the decision is now out of your hands. It is in the hands of the provincial and therefore--one's faith must accept--in the hands of God.

This is the second act of faith.

Like any proposal, one's request to enter the Society can be rejected or deferred. As with a marriage proposal, such a response doesn't mean one is not a good man. It doesn't even mean that the girl does not love him. It merely means that, for any or all of a thousand reasons, he is not the "right" one. Still, no matter how levelheaded or tough a man is, there is no way that such a response is easy to take. But again, as with a marriage proposal, the only sensible response is to wipe away the tears, dust off your hands, say "Well, that one's settled," and go out looking for another girl.

If a man is deferred, that does not mean that he has been rejected. It merely means that for the moment the Society is not sure that being a Jesuit will be the best life for him. It's suggesting that he go to college for awhile, live a little, toughen up a bit or soften down a bit or whatever. The wisest advice for men who have been deferred is to keep on living like any other college man, not as a monk-in-the-world. He should keep in contact with an advisor, keep praying, but still go to dances, date, run with the boys, since very often deferrals are based on the fact that he has not really done enough of that before. After a year or two, if he still feels that he belongs in the Society, he need only apply again without going through the whole admissions process again.

If a man is accepted, I need say nothing. At that moment he is in better hands than mine. I can only join with my betters, Ignatius, Brebeuf, Carl Hausmann, and all those unknown men who will feed his growing vocation and with them say, "Welcome."

Bibliography

History of the Society of Jesus

Bangert, William, S.J. A History of the Society of Jesus. St.
Louis: Institute of Jesuit Sources, 1972.
Brodrick, James, S.J. The Origin of the Jesuits. New York:
Longmans, Green & Co. , 1940.
_____. The Progress of the Jesuits. New York: Longmans,
Green & Co. , 1947.
Harney, Martin, S.J. The Jesuits in History. Chicago: Loyola
University Press, 1962.
Hollis, Christopher. The Jesuits: A History. New York:
Macmillan, 1968.
Meadows, Denis. A Popular History of the Jesuits. New York:
Macmillan, 1958.

St. Ignatius Loyola

Brodrick, James, S.J. St. Ignatius Loyola: The Pilgrim Years.
New York: Farrar, Straus & Cudahy, 1956.
Doncoeur, Paul, S.J. The Heart of Ignatius. Baltimore: Helicon,
1959.
Dudon, Paul, S.J. St. Ignatius of Loyola. Milwaukee: Bruce,
1949.
Papasogli, Giorgio, S.J. St. Ignatius of Loyola. Staten Island,
New York: Society of St. Paul, 1959.
Rahner, Hugo, S.J. St. Ignatius of Loyola. Chicago: Regnery,
1956.

Collected Biographies

Basset, Bernard, S.J. The English Jesuits. London: Burns &
Oates, 1968.
LaFarge, John, S.J. A Report on the American Jesuits. New
York: Farrar, Straus & Cudahy, 1956.
Leary, John, S.J. Better a Day. New York: Macmillan, 1951.
_____. I Lift My Lamp: Jesuits in America. Westminster,
Maryland: Newman Press, 1955.
Nash, Robert, S.J. Jesuits. Westminster, Maryland: Newman
Press, 1956.

Individual Biographies

Brebeuf   Talbot, Francis, S.J. Saint Among the Hurons.
             Garden City, New York: Doubleday, 1956.
Campion   Waugh, Evelyn. Edmund Campion. Boston: Little,
             Brown & Co., 1948.
Ciszek   Ciszek, Walter, S.J. With God in Russia. New
             York: McGraw-Hill, 1964.

211

Gerard   Gerard, John, S.J. Autobiography of a Hunted
              Priest. Garden City, New York: Doubleday,
              1952.
Hopkins   Weyand, Norman, S.J., ed. Immortal Diamond:
              Studies in Gerard Manley Hopkins. New York:
              Sheed and Ward, 1949.
Kino   Bolton, Herbert. The Padre on Horseback.
              Chicago: Loyola University Press, 1963.
Lord   Lord, Daniel, S.J. Played by Ear. Chicago:
              Loyola University Press, 1956.
O'Callahan   O'Callahan, Joseph, S.J. I Was Chaplain on the
              Franklin. New York: Macmillan, 1956.
Pro   Royer, Franchon. Padre Pro. New York: Kenedy,
              1954.
Ricci   Cronin, Vincent. Wise Man from the West. New
              York: E. P. Dutton & Co., 1955.
Teilhard   Cuenot, Claude. Teilhard de Chardin. Baltimore:
              Helicon, 1965.
Xavier   Brodrick, James, S.J. St. Francis Xavier. New
              York: Pellegrini & Cudahy, 1952.

American Jesuit Provincial Offices

California Province, serving Arizona, California, Hawaii, Nevada, and Utah.

Provincial House
P. O. Box 519
Los Gatos, California 95030
(408) 354-6143

Chicago Province, serving northern Illinois, Indiana, Kentucky, and southern Ohio.

Provincial Residence
509 North Oak Park Avenue
Oak Park, Illinois 60302
(312) 626-7934

Detroit Province, serving Michigan and northern Ohio.

Provincial Offices
602 Boulevard Center Building
Cass and West Grand Boulevard
Detroit, Michigan 48202
(313) 871-2131

French Canada, serving Montreal, Quebec, and Sudbury.

Maison Provinciale
25 ouest, rue Jarry
Montreal H2P 1S6
(514) 387-2541

Maryland Province, serving Delaware, District of Columbia,
Maryland, southern New Jersey, North Carolina, Pennsylvania, Virginia, and West Virginia.

Provincial Residence
5704 Roland Avenue
Baltimore, Maryland 21210
(301) 435-1833

Missouri Province, serving Colorado, southern Illinois,
Kansas, Missouri, Oklahoma, and Wyoming.

Provincial Residence
4511 West Pine Boulevard
St. Louis, Missouri 63108
(314) 361-7765

New England Province, serving Connecticut, Maine, Massachusetts, New Hampshire, Rhode Island, and Vermont.

Provincial Offices
393 Commonwealth Avenue
Boston, Massachusetts 02115
(617) 266-7233

New Orleans Province, serving Alabama, Arkansas, Florida, Georgia, Louisiana, Mississippi, New Mexico, South Carolina, Tennessee, and Texas.

Provincial Residence
6301 Stratford Place, P. O. Box 6378
New Orleans, Louisiana 70174
(504) 394-2411

New York Province, serving northern New Jersey and New York.

Provincial Offices
501 East Fordham Road
Bronx, New York 10458
(212) 584-0300

Oregon Province, serving Alaska, Idaho, Montana, Oregon, and Washington.

Provincial House
2222 N. W. Hoyt
Portland, Oregon 97210
(503) 226-6977

Upper Canada, serving Canada except Montreal and Quebec.

Provincial Residence
2 Hawthorn Gardens
Toronto, Ontario M4W 1P3
(416) 922-5168

Wisconsin Province, serving Iowa, Minnesota, Nebraska,
   North Dakota, South Dakota, and Wisconsin.

Provincial Offices
2120 West Clybourn Street
Suite 200
Milwaukee, Wisconsin 53233
(414) 344-7464